THOUGHTS ON SOME QUESTIONS RELATING TO WOMEN, 1860–1908

AMS PRESS
NEW YORK

THOUGHTS ON SOME QUESTIONS RELATING TO WOMEN, 1860–1908

BY

EMILY DAVIES, LL.D.

WITH PREFATORY NOTE

BY

E. E. CONSTANCE JONES

MISTRESS OF GIRTON COLLEGE, CAMBRIDGE

CAMBRIDGE : BOWES AND BOWES

1910

Library of Congress Cataloging in Publication Data

Davies, Emily, 1830–1921.
   Thoughts on some questions relating to women,
1860–1908.

   (Women of letters)
   CONTENTS: Letters to a daily paper, Newcastle-on
-Tyne.--Female physicians.--Employment of women.
--Medicine as a profession for women. ₍etc.₎
   1. Education of women--Great Britain--History.
2. Women in medicine--History. 3. Woman--Suffrage--
History. I. Title. II. Series.
LC2042.D38 1973   301.41'2'0942   73-14557
0-404-56741-X

Reprinted from the edition of 1910, Cambridge
First AMS edition published, 1973
Manufactured in the United States of America

AMS PRESS, INC.
New York, N.Y.   10003

mw

PREFATORY NOTE

THE following papers are selected from writings published by Miss Emily Davies during the years 1860—1908. They are arranged in chronological order, and, with the exception of a few omissions, are reproduced as first issued, without alteration. The Letters addressed to a Newcastle daily paper were reprinted as a pamphlet entitled *Thoughts on some Questions relating to Women*. This title has been adopted for the present volume as indicating its general tenour. The chief topics are given more in detail in the table of contents, and as regards the treatment under each head the papers speak for themselves. It may, however, not be out of place to draw attention to the very interesting way in which a perusal of these writings impresses upon the reader the stages of development of that movement for the advancement of women in which Miss Davies took such an important part; and in initiating and fostering which, there was the fullest scope for the faith and insight, the courage and tenacity, without which failure would have been inevitable. It is the genuinely historical nature of the evidence that makes this quite uncalculated reflection of the spirit of the time, in each paper as it was written, such a striking record—a record of a continuous and profound, and yet unobtrusive, change in the general outlook in matters relating to women. The opening

of University Local Examinations to girls in 1865—
the starting at Hitchin in 1869 of the "New College
for Women" (transferred to Girton in 1873), and
the founding of other Women's Colleges*—the formal
opening of Cambridge Degree Examinations in
1881, following the admission of women to the
membership and degrees of the University of
London in 1878—these are among the landmarks in
an epoch-making development. But a recital even
of all the conspicuous steps in the advance, as shown
in school and college education, the opening of the
medical profession, the possibilities of recognised
and important civic service, would altogether fail to
give an adequate idea of the enormous change in the
life of women which we owe to this movement—a
revolution carried through so quietly and irresistibly,
that now, as we look back, it is seen to exhibit the
essential characteristics of a true evolution.

To Miss Davies belongs the high honour of having
been one of the pioneers who actually led and guided
the advance. What a transformation it has effected
in education and opportunities can be estimated best
by those who know both what the condition of things
was forty or fifty years ago, and what it is now; they
only can appreciate to the full all that is due to the
workers in this far-reaching reform. How many a
sympathetic mother in the old days has said, or
thought, of a daughter eager to learn, "What a pity
she is not a boy, that she might go to College!"
Now, the hunger for knowledge need no longer be a
tragedy merely because it happens to occur in a

* See pp. 197—200.

daughter; and those women who have known the joy of intellectual satisfaction and development, and of the exercise of trained capacity and intelligent social service at present possible, cannot but feel that they owe a debt of gratitude, too great for payment and too deep for words, to the nineteenth-century pioneers.

The work is not yet completed. It is for the later generations to carry it on to further and fuller development—with the same high aims, the same untiring zeal, and the same temperate wisdom by which the Women's Movement has from its earliest days been so honourably distinguished.

E. E. CONSTANCE JONES.

GIRTON COLLEGE,
  CAMBRIDGE,
    May, 1910.

CONTENTS

QUESTIONS RELATING TO WOMEN

Letters addressed to a Daily Paper at Newcastle-upon-Tyne, 1860

I

In a recent charge to the Grand Jury of Hull, the Recorder, Mr. S. Warren, expressed himself as follows: —" Human ingenuity could hardly more admirably occupy itself, than in discovering and devising new and creditable modes of occupation for females, especially the younger ones, of the middle classes. The sufferings and exposure to dangers of the worst kind—the griefs and anxieties of overburdened families, which might thus be averted, would richly reward a persevering philanthropist." In these words Mr. Warren gave utterance to thoughts that are at this time occupying the minds of many; and yet probably, few of us have considered so seriously as the question deserves, what young women are actually doing. We take for granted in a general way that they are doing something, or might be, if they liked, but we really do not know what. The fact is, that those who are not compelled by necessity to labour for their maintenance, are discouraged—partly by

1

conventional prejudices, and partly by the difficulty
of finding employment suited to their powers—from
applying themselves to settled work of any kind.
Take the case of a young girl just entering, or rather
who should be just entering, upon the business of
life. She has spent a few years at school, has learnt
the rudiments of French, can play on the piano, and
is tolerably skilful with her needle. She can read
and write—whether she can also spell, and work a
sum correctly and quickly, is doubtful, as too many
parents are more anxious for proficiency in what are
called accomplishments than in these fundamentals
which make no show. She is released from the
wholesome discipline of school, and thrown suddenly
upon her own resources. Her mother probably
expects her to help a little in household matters,
which occupy her for, perhaps, two hours of the day,
and the rest of her time is thrown upon her hands,
to spend as she likes. Can we wonder that her days
are passed in laborious trifling, and her nights in
dissipation? Far be it from me to say that she does
nothing. She would probably tell you that she is
so busy she really does not know what to do first.
There are notes that *must* be written, calls that
must be returned, visits that *must* be paid, and a
hundred other *musts*, all of which would vanish in a
moment before the breath of a real necessity. And
so the months go round. If she marries, the arrangement answers tolerably well—not too well, for such
a life of busy idleness is not the best preparation for
the cares and responsibilities of a wife and mother.

But if she does not marry? Or if, through misfortune or by the sickness, or death, or misconduct, of her husband, the duty of providing for herself and her children devolves upon her, what can she do? Relations and kind friends take counsel together, and after much deliberation it is decided that Miss or Mrs. ―― must either find a situation as governess, or keep a school. She is not fond of teaching, it is true, and she has had no training for it, and the little she once knew she has forgotten; but, after all, people must adapt themselves to their circumstances, and if her terms are low enough she will get pupils. Of the laborious days with scanty earnings, implied in such a decision, it is not necessary here to speak; the hardships of governess-life are proverbial. But there is another aspect of the question which has, I think, received less attention than it deserves. I refer to the injury done to children by putting their education into unskilful hands. It seems to be taken for granted that anybody can educate, and so the honourable office of training the young comes to be looked upon as a mere money-getting speculation, in which puffing, canvassing, and other tricks of trade, are unblushingly practised. The few who take a higher view of their duties, who look upon their office as a sacred calling, not to be lightly dealt with, are confounded with the ignorant and unfit, and our children suffer. And this, not because people are unwilling to pay for the education of their children, but because women who have no vocation for teaching are forced by necessity into a profession for which

3

they are unsuited. It may be fairly objected, indeed, that parents have the matter in their own hands, and are not obliged to give their children into the charge of persons whom they consider incompetent. But if a reasonable discrimination were at all commonly practised, how deplorable would be the condition of many governesses! Their one resource would be taken from them, and beggary or starvation would be their only alternative.

The case of unmarried women " not obliged to do anything," is, at first sight, and in many respects, far less urgent and distressing. But in one point of view, those who are compelled to work have the advantage. The spur of hard necessity, at least, brings out some energy, and awakens some activity, while those whose daily bread is brought to them, without a thought on their part, having no pressing motive to exertion, and being unable to " discover or devise " any " new and creditable mode of occupation for females," in too many cases merely fill up their time as best they may, in the practice of the various arts known under the general name of fancy-work. The labourers are standing idle in the market-place, because no man hath hired them. I am aware that I shall here be met with the objection, that in a community like our own, and in most large towns, the difficulty is not to find work, but to find labourers; that there is abundant employment for all, in visiting the poor, in the management of schools, and in other works of charity. In answer to this, I beg leave to submit, that all women are not made to be philanthropists. It would be considered unreasonable to expect that all men should take Holy Orders, or enrol themselves as town missionaries, and it is equally unreasonable to expect that all women should engage in similar work. Indeed, as a general rule, young unmarried women are not the best fitted for the office of counselling their neighbours, and it is by this class that the discipline of some steady work is most needed. I do not say that they are always conscious of the want. People in general, I fancy, do pretty much what is expected of them, and so long as it is the theory of society, that the whole duty of woman is to "go gracefully idle," it is not likely that ordinary women will disturb the peace of their neighbours by passionate appeals for work. But the want is not the less pressing where it is not felt, and society cannot afford to disregard it. It is usual to treat this as a mere woman's question, and we hear now and then of women's rights and women's wrongs. I believe the best women think more of duties and responsibilities than of rights and wrongs, and care comparatively little for any "right" but that of giving their best in the service of God and humanity, by the free development of whatever capacities of usefulness they possess; and if, by our narrow conventional notions and social prejudices, we deny this just claim, it is not women only who are wronged. They may indeed suffer from what Coleridge calls "the obscure trouble of a baffled instinct," but they do not suffer alone. That which

God hath joined, man cannot put asunder:

> "The woman's cause is man's; they rise or sink
> Together, dwarf'd or godlike, bond or free;
> For she that out of Lethe scales with man
> The shining steps of Nature, shares with man
> His nights, his days, moves with him to one goal,
> Stays all the fair young planet in her hands—
> If she be small, slight-natured, miserable,
> How shall men grow?"

Frivolity is not harmless. So far as its influence extends, it works for evil, and the absence of any definite settled occupation, about which it is not a mere matter of choice from hour to hour whether to do it or leave it undone, is in itself calculated to encourage a trifling habit of mind, injurious not only to the women who indulge in it, but to every one with whom they have to do. To bring about a more healthy state of things is surely an object worth trying for. The means by which we may hope to attain it, will make the subject of a future letter.

II

In considering the various means by which the present condition of women may be improved, the most obvious is that of extending the range of occupations open to them. It is manifestly necessary, however, to make at the same time some change in the mode of their education, as they are unable, under the system at present pursued, to accept a position, even when offered, in which special preparatory training is required. These two operations must, so to speak, dovetail together, and, this being the case, it is clear that the task must be accomplished by the general public, not by any particular class alone. It has been said, indeed, that women have the matter in their own hands; and I have little doubt that if a large number of women were to unite in an energetic demand for an enlarged sphere of work, backing up their claim with satisfactory evidence of fitness, they would meet with ready attention, and their admission into many offices from which they are now excluded would be a question only of time. The superior cheapness of their labour would recommend them to employers uninfluenced by any higher motive. But it seems to be forgotten, that women are, happily, not a class apart. They are acted upon by all the influences which give an impress to public opinion, and *young* women are especially bound by the conventional usages of society. It is, therefore, as unlikely as it would be undesirable, that women should unite in a separate movement, even for the attainment of an object in which they are the parties more immediately interested. I say immediately, for, as has been before remarked, the whole community is concerned, more or less directly, in the solution of this question. There is one class, however, with whom rests the largest share of the power, as well as of the responsibility. I refer to the parents of daughters, and to them I would appeal. Let them well understand, once for all, that their daughters, as they grow up, will have faculties to be developed, understandings to be cultivated and turned to account, and that it is the duty of parents to help and guide them in the choice of a field for the useful exercise of their talents. Let them pass under review the various departments of labour hitherto unoccupied by women, and carefully weigh the advantages and disadvantages of each particular sphere of exertion, always bearing in mind, that, in choosing a trade or profession for a girl, there is to be considered not only what she is able to do, but what will be most useful to her hereafter, should she be called upon to fulfil the duties of a wife and mother. The guidance of a family is a calling which will never become obsolete, and whose importance should never be overlooked. Let us consider whether there are not some occupations, the training for which would help women to do their duty in any state of life, be it married or single, into which it should please God to call them.

In Mr. Ward's Trades' Directory for Newcastle I find enumerated no less than 320 different trades and professions. Of these, many are manifestly unsuited to women; others are equally inappropriate to men. There remains a considerable proportion which might with propriety be pursued by both sexes.

To begin with what may be looked upon as the highest class in the social scale—that of owners of landed property. Not many women are to be found in this category, and among the few, still fewer retain the management of their affairs in their own hands. It is generally confided to a brother or uncle, or in default of any male relation, an agent is employed. Sometimes the deputy does his work well, sometimes not. In either case, the really responsible person is kept idle, forfeiting the benefit of the moral and intellectual education which the possession of property ought to imply, out of deference to the received idea that women "do not understand business." It is indeed true that many women do not, but is it also true that they cannot understand business? In the few instances in which the experiment has been tried, experience seems to prove the contrary. One instance will doubtless occur to many of your readers, of a lady in our own locality, of high rank and noble birth, who, being in the order of Providence left a widow in the possession of large estates, including some of the most extensive collieries in the North of England, thought it no shame to accept the responsibilities thus devolving upon her, and who has discharged the duties of her stewardship with a zeal and perseverance, and a conscientious regard to the best interests of those connected with her, well worthy of imitation, as those who have the best opportunities of knowing can testify. Other examples on a smaller scale might be adduced—all tending to prove that women have no natural incapacity for business, provided only that they have been trained to habits of accuracy and order—habits which can never be useless in any condition of life.

Among the learned professions, that of medicine might be advantageously practised by both men and women. It is an art for which many women have a marked natural predilection, showing itself in their eagerness to prescribe for their friends and neighbours. They seem determined to be doctors, whether we will or no, and the only question to be decided is, Shall they be ignorant empirics or thoroughly-educated practitioners? We laugh at their fancy for doctoring, as a harmless weakness: is it not rather a divinely implanted instinct which we should do well to cultivate and improve? I believe that in imparting to a young woman a sound scientific medical education we should be bestowing a gift which would be of infinite value, whatever might be her lot in life. If she should marry, such a knowledge of medicine would enable her to prescribe wisely for her children and servants; if she should remain single, she would be free to exercise her talent for the benefit of women and children in general. There is no doubt that, as a rule, women would prefer the services of physicians of their own sex; and a well-qualified practitioner would have plenty of patients. But there are at present great and almost insuperable difficulties in the way of obtaining the necessary education in England. It is a fact, I believe, that the only female physician legally registered in this country—Elizabeth Blackwell, M.D.—was obliged to obtain the greater part of her instruction elsewhere, and, though herself an Englishwoman, she is indebted to an American college for her degree. There is reason to hope, however, that the prejudices of medical authorities are gradually giving way, and that ere long they will be prepared to aid women in the acquirement of a thorough knowledge of a science which, as mothers and nurses, they are already so frequently called upon to practise.

In passing from the professions to the counting-house and manufactory, we find that the question, Have women a place here—has already been solved in individual cases. Large concerns have prospered under the direction of women, and it may be considered as proved by experience that it is possible for a woman to manage a business without injury to her "distinctive womanhood." It is certainly not easy to see why it should be unfeminine for a girl to sit in her father's office, under his immediate eye (and protection if needed), gradually acquiring experience which may, in process of time, when she arrives at years of discretion, enable her to take his place and relieve him of the anxiety which so often presses upon lóving fathers, who feel themselves growing old with a family inadequately provided for. Nor would her time have been thrown away, looked upon as a preparation for married life. Though as a wife she would cease to work in the counting-house, the habit of work and the experience in business would make her more able to administer the affairs of her household, and would keep her from being a helpless burden in case of misfortune or widowhood. It ought to be understood, however, that a daughter should be paid for her services, like any other clerk, according to their value. A mere dilettante "helping papa a little with his accounts," would be no discipline; it would be only one more added to the many expedients already in use for killing a girl's time.

The trades may be divided into two departments, that of production and that of retail. It would be difficult to mention any trade in which a woman could not sell as well as a man, provided she has the necessary knowledge of book-keeping, and a capacity, to be acquired by experience, of judging of the quality of her goods. The employment of shop-women is becoming more common every day, and it is probable that before many years elapse, women will also be admitted to the management of shops, especially of some which seem to be their peculiar province, such as those of drapers, hosiers, &c. But the manufacturing department is much less accessible. It is scarcely credible, though I am afraid true, that at this moment it would be useless to ask a respect-able hairdresser to take a female apprentice. And yet, surely, of all arts, that of cutting and curling ladies' hair, and manufacturing frizettes, is the least masculine. I believe that, with a few exceptions, there would be a similar reluctance on the part of chemists and druggists to initiate a female appren-tice into the mysteries of their craft, though as a sort of scientific cookery, if I may be allowed the expression, it would not seem out of place in female hands. The experiment of a printing office, entirely managed by women, has been tried in London, and is thoroughly successful. Carving and gilding, enamelling, and other arts in which manual skill is chiefly required, have also been proposed.

It would occupy too much space to enumerate all the branches of manufacture which might occupy the hands and brains of women, and it is unnecessary to pursue this part of the subject farther. I am aware that many objections, reasonable and unreasonable, may be urged against the carrying out of the foregoing suggestions. I have purposely avoided referring to these objections in passing, feeling that they are too numerous and too serious to be dismissed with a casual notice. I therefore propose to consider them separately in a final communication.

III

The arguments brought forward against the employment of women in fields of labour hitherto closed against them, are so various, and in some instances, so confused and mutually contradictory, that it is somewhat difficult to state them fairly. I believe, however, that almost all the current objections are based upon one or other of these two assumptions: either, that the proposed changes are undesirable in an economical point of view; or, that they are objectionable on moral and social grounds. To begin with the first class. It is said that the labour market is already amply supplied, and that by the introduction of more workers, the rate of wages would be lowered, by which the whole community would suffer. If this were so, it would at least be fair that all should suffer alike, and not that, as now, the heaviest share of the burden should be

borne by the weaker sex. But is not the whole
argument based upon a fallacy? It seems to be
forgotten that whether women work or not, they
must exist, and if they are not allowed to labour
with their hands the thing that is good, they must
be burdensome to society. Nothing is saved by
keeping them inactive, and the produce of their
labour is lost. No man in his senses would keep
two or three of his sons doing nothing, in order to
give the rest a better chance of getting on; yet this
would be as reasonable as to refuse work to women
lest there should not be enough left for men. If the
labour market should become overstocked, it would
be necessary to seek fresh outlets; and it seems
likely that the colonies will supply openings for
both men and women during many years to come.
I do not think, however, that the admission of
women into certain trades and professions, from
which they are now excluded, would perceptibly
affect the general rate of wages. It should be borne
in mind that female workers would be continually
drafted off by marriage, and that consequently the
number of additional competitors would not be very
formidable.

This brings me to another argument, which
is so reasonable that I am anxious to give it
full consideration. It is urged that as, in the great
majority of cases, women would give up their
business on entering upon that other business of
marriage, it is not worth while to throw away
upon them an expensive preparation for anything

else. I reply, that the training of clerks is not expensive. They learn by experience, for which they do not pay in money. Capital is no doubt required to set up in trade, but even that expenditure could scarcely be looked upon as thrown away, as it is generally easy to dispose of a business, supposing there is no other member of the family to succeed to it. The money spent in preparing for the medical profession is sunk, but a few years of practice would probably repay the actual cost, and to the mother of a family it would, to a great extent, be made up by saving the expense of a family doctor. The Rev. Charles Simeon is reported to have said to a friend, "If you have a thousand pounds to give your son, put it in his head rather than in his pocket." The advice is equally applicable to the case of daughters. Give them an education which in case of need they can turn to some profitable account, rather than invest the savings destined for their use in the Funds, or in joint-stock banks, those attractive but dangerous concerns, whose downfall from time to time brings ruin on hundreds of helpless women.

The objectors to an extension of the sphere of women, on moral and social grounds, take a different line of argument. It is contended by some that a certain degree of helplessness in women is not only becoming but useful, as a stimulus to exertion in men. This is scarcely a fair argument, unless it could be proved that it is also good for women to sit with folded hands admiring the activity of men. I believe, however, that it is in itself without foundation. Single men do not feel stimulated by the vague knowledge that there are a good many women in the world requiring to be supported, and married men would in any case have their families to provide for. A fear has indeed been expressed that, if women had anything else to do, they would be unwilling to marry, and a diminution in the number of marriages (justly regarded as a serious evil), would ensue. But those who entertain such an apprehension must surely look upon matrimony as a very unhappy estate. If women can only be driven into it by *ennui*, or as a means of earning a livelihood, how is it that men are willing to marry? Are the advantages all on their side? The experience of happy wives and mothers forbids such a supposition. It is likely, on the contrary, that, by making women more capable, the number of marriages would be increased, as many men would be glad to marry, who are now deterred from doing so by prudential considerations.

There remains one more objection, which, I believe, lies at the root of all. It is averred that "public life" is injurious to women; that they are meant for the domestic circle; and that, though we are bound to sympathise with, and relieve to the extent of our ability, cases of individual suffering, we must on no account interfere with the law of nature, which has made home, and home only, woman's sphere. It is most true that no advantages, real or apparent, to be gained in public life would compensate for the loss of the domestic virtues; but does it necessarily follow that, if women took a more active part in the business of the world, they would therefore cease to care for home? Let us look at this bugbear—this *bête-noire* called "public life"—fairly in the face. What is it we mean by it? Is there any woman living who does not go more or less into public; and what is it that makes the difference between justifiable and unjustifiable publicity? Probably no woman in the three kingdoms leads a more public life than the Queen, yet it may be questioned whether a more admirable wife and mother is to be found among her subjects. The work of a medical practitioner is scarcely more public than that of a district visitor; the head of a manufacturing firm may lead as private a life as the head of a millinery establishment; the business of a chemist and druggist is no more public than that of a confectioner. The fact is, that "to us, the fools of habit," what is new is dangerous; what we have long been accustomed to, is proper and becoming. Fathers who would shake their heads at the idea of taking their daughters into their own counting-houses, allow them to stand behind a stall at a bazaar, or to lead off at a charity ball—far more public scenes, and where, indeed, publicity is essential to success. And if we really hold the doctrine that it is improper for a woman to follow any calling which cannot be pursued at her own fireside, how is it that we flock to hear public singers? It is idle to say that we would not allow our own daughters or sisters to perform in public. We have no right to sanction by our presence, and to derive enjoyment from the exercise of, a profession which in theory we condemn as unfeminine and, if so, of a demoralising tendency.

In conclusion, I may be permitted to say a few words to those liberal-minded persons who are favourable to the movement now in progress, but who content themselves with standing aside and wishing it God-speed, under the impression that that is all they can do. You can—nay, you must—either help this movement forward, or, in a greater or less degree, retard it. If you are a medical man, you can throw the weight of your influence into the scale in favour of extending to women the educational advantages you have yourself enjoyed; if you are a merchant or a banker, you may be able to make such arrangements in your office as would render it practicable to employ female clerks and cashiers; if you are a master-tradesman, you can make known your willingness to receive female apprentices; if you take part in the government of hospitals, prisons, &c., you can encourage the increased employment of women as officers in these and kindred institutions. Whoever and whatever you are, you can testify against the notion that indolence is feminine and refined; and that if a lady may, in certain cases, be permitted to work, her labour must at any rate be unpaid. You can assist in breaking down those false notions of propriety by which women are hampered in so many directions. And so you may help them to exchange a condition of labour without profit, and leisure without ease, for a life of wholesome activity, and the repose that comes with fruitful toil.

Female Physicians.

[*The English Woman's Journal*, 1861.]

THE elaborate and apparently well-considered observations of "A Physician of twenty-one years'
standing," in the English Woman's Journal of last
month, call for some notice on the part of those who
believe the medical profession to be a sphere of
usefulness especially suited to women.

Your correspondent, after expressing his general
sympathy with the efforts made for the "expansion
of woman's responsibilities and work," proceeds to
remark, that "we shall fail in our attempts if they
are not consonant with those laws of our physical
and moral nature which are the necessary basis upon
which alone any ethical or political structure can be
raised, that shall not prove the mere 'baseless fabric
of a vision.'" Is it not the question in dispute,
whether there is anything in the practice of medicine
by women which must necessarily contravene these
laws?

"A Physician" asks us to consider the question
under two aspects, corresponding to two main
elements which determine the choice of a young
man in selecting a profession: his own aptitude,
and the sphere into which his profession may throw
him.

First, as to aptitude, by which I conceive is meant a general liking for some particular pursuit, combined with a certain amount of ability. I scarcely suppose that the most vehement objectors to female physicians would argue that, as a class, women have less taste for Medicine than men. An ignorant love of doctoring is one of the recognised weaknesses of women. Their intellectual and physical incapacity requires to be proved by " something more stringent than the dogmatic opinion of any writer." Whether the mental powers of women are on the whole equal to those of men is a wide and difficult question, on which it is needless to enter, inasmuch as we claim only the right to exercise such powers as we possess, be they great or small. "A Physician" speaks of the previous training medical students have received as boys, as if it were impossible that girls should receive the same. But is not some training of this sort just what women want? On this point, I may be allowed to quote from a well-known author :—

"Women's education must be made such as to ensure some accuracy and reasoning. This may be done with any subject of education, and is done with men, whatever they learn, because they are expected to produce and use their acquirements. But the greatest object of intellectual education, the improvement of the mental powers, is as needful for one sex as the other, and requires the same means in both sexes. The same accuracy, attention, logic, and method, that are attempted in the education of men, should be aimed at in that of women."

And again :—

"It is a narrow view of things to suppose that a just cultivation of women's mental powers will take them out of their sphere,—it will only enlarge that sphere. The most cultivated women perform their common duties best. They see more in those duties. They can do more. Lady Jane Grey would, I dare say, have bound up a wound or managed a household with any unlearned woman of her day. Queen Elizabeth did manage a kingdom; and we find no pedantry in her way of doing it." *

That lady students, entering upon the course without preliminary training, do so at an immense disadvantage, we are quite ready to admit. It is perhaps the strongest point in our case, as regards mere power, both physical and intellectual, that women have been able to do so much while debarred from the advantages of early education open to most men.

"Supposing the difficulties of the student's life surpassed, you then come to the troubles and difficulties of incipient practice." And here the physical weakness of women is the argument. That, as a whole, men are stronger than women, no one denies; but does that justify us in assuming that every individual man is stronger than any individual woman? We learn from "A Physician" what our own observation confirms, that many members of the medical profession are feeble in constitution and scarcely fit

* "Friends in Council," Book I. p. 142

for the struggle of life; but we do not therefore condemn them to complete inaction, nor do we propose any regulation for limiting the profession to men of herculean frames. On the other hand, we learn from our own observation, though not from your correspondent, that in various parts of the country women of the lower classes go through an amount of labour under which a gentleman would probably break down. I have myself been told by an eye-witness, that in Staffordshire, women are doing, "not men's work, but horses' work;" and it is an unquestionable fact, that in manufactories where women and girls are employed, the low, rough, exhausting work is given over to them, while the higher branches, in which some intelligence is required, are reserved for men. The same may be said of brick-making and other laborious out-door work. Let it not be supposed that we look with satisfaction upon this overtasking of the physical strength of women. On the contrary, we believe that by opening out occupations in which intelligence goes for something, these poor degraded women may gradually be drawn up from a condition in which common morality is almost an impossibility; and so, while delivering the upper classes from the curse of idleness, we may at the same time effectually help those least able to help themselves. But we do think that while women are showing themselves to be capable of such an amount of physical exertion, the comparatively far easier career of a physician should not be closed to us on the ground of physical weakness. It is remarked,

Female Physicians

that "unless she can cope with men in all the various branches of medical inquiry and practice, she will, in the race of life, necessarily go to the wall; and the struggle, which will be unavoidable, must be to the stronger." Be it so. Women are so much in the habit of going to the wall, that the position will not alarm them by its novelty, and their fate will only be the same as that of all members of the profession who are not able to cope on equal terms with their superior brethren.

As we look round upon medical men, we cannot help observing many physicians and surgeons who do not appear to be superior in ability to average women; and as for many years, only women somewhat above the average in mental and physical strength will dare to think of entering the profession, perhaps they would *not* always go to the wall. At any rate, their position could scarcely be worse than that of governesses. A practice of four or five hundred a year is not thought much of among physicians; but ladies, who can seldom, even by hard work during their best years, earn more than, say, £200 a year, will not despise the crumbs which fall from the rich man's table.

"A Physician" proceeds to inquire, "Is there a proper field for the employment and support of female physicians?" We unhesitatingly reply that all diseases to which women and children are liable would naturally come within the province of the female physician, and surely that is a domain wide enough, without encroaching upon the sphere of men. But your correspondent is confident that ladies would not consult female doctors. On this point my experience is widely different from his. I can well believe that ladies, being suddenly questioned, would reply at once that they would not have confidence in a woman. Hastily assuming that the female physician would be either a shallow, superficially taught lady, or a sort of superior nurse, they naturally feel that they would prefer the services of an able and experienced man. But ladies who have had time to think, are almost unanimous in declaring that if they could secure the attendance of equally well-educated women (and this can be certified by a Degree), they would give them the preference. I speak not from hearsay, but from actual personal knowledge, when I say that this feeling is much stronger among refined women of the poorer classes, who are more at the mercy of young men and the inferior order of practitioners. The feeling is strongest of all among young girls. I believe that to many of them the sympathy and tenderness of a woman would be absolutely more curative than the possibly superior skill of a man— of which, indeed, they often refuse to avail themselves.

Finally, your correspondent inquires from whence you would draw your supply of females who are to study medicine and become physicians? To which I reply, from whence do we draw our supply of governesses? Of them there appears to be an abundant, nay an excessive, supply. A female medical student need not "devote herself heart and soul to celibacy." She might indeed exercise a more independent choice, because she would not be driven into marriage by the mere longing for some satisfying occupation; but if suitable marriage came in her way, her profession need be no hindrance. To have passed a few years in patient study and earnest work would surely be an admirable preparation for married life; and she would be better off than other women, in having a profession to fall back upon in case of widowhood or other misfortune. This question of marriage, in fact, amounts to this,—Are all women to be shut out from any and every method of earning money by honest and intelligent work lest they should grow too independent of their natural supporters, or are they to be encouraged and urged to use their gifts as those who must give account? It is beginning to be believed that women have certain gifts of hand, and that it is not unfeminine to use them. Let us hope that in a generation or two it will also be admitted that they have heads, and that this being so, it is their bounden duty "sincerely to give a true account of their gift of reason, to the benefit and use of men." How they may best labour to this end, can surely be satisfactorily proved only by experience. There may be much confident assertion on both sides, but till the experiment has been fairly tried, we have no right to decide positively that women can or cannot go through the medical course uninjured; that they will or will not find patients. And if ladies show some reluctance in coming forward as students, let us not hastily draw unfavourable conclusions. We are reminded by your correspondent that the training must commence in early life; and it would be folly to expect that girls of sixteen will eagerly press for admission into a profession, "into which," as they are told by "A Physician of twenty-one years' standing," "they are to be forced against the dictates of nature and all the usages and requirements of society." They may indeed suspect that their interest and delight in medical study and in doctoring (not merely nursing) is in itself a "dictate of nature," and that "the usages of society" are in this case, as they have sometimes been before, unreasonable and wrong. But modest, well-brought up girls are slow—can we wish them to be less so?—to act upon their own convictions against the authority of their more experienced friends, and for them to enter upon such a struggle unaided would be clearly impossible. On the other hand, women, whose convictions have grown with their growth, and who have arrived at an age at which they are at liberty to judge for themselves, find it too late to enter upon the medical course. The spring and energy which might have been turned to account for the service of God and man has been exhausted, frittered away in desultory, unsatisfying effort, if it has not found an outlet for itself in actual mischief.

Your correspondent candidly admits, that "You know, and the readers of this Journal know, the female heart better than he can." It is indeed so.

Female Physicians

Men, the most liberal and the most generous, do not know, and never will know, what women are suffering, who, to the eye of the world, are "very happy." Young ladies are not all so thoughtless as they seem. The injunction to "make themselves happy" in luxurious idleness, is as much a mockery to them as to Rasselas and Neyakah in the Happy Valley. To such happiness, unblessed of God and unhonoured of men, may they never learn to reconcile themselves.

Northumberland and Durham Branch of the Society for promoting the employment of women, 1861.

On the 24th of October, 1860, a meeting was held at the house of the Mayor of Newcastle-upon-Tyne, at which the following resolution was proposed and carried:—"That a Committee be formed in aid of the Society for promoting the employment of women, consisting of the ladies here present; and that the objects of the Committee be, to receive subscriptions, gather and diffuse information, and to encourage by personal influence, the introduction of women into such occupations as are suitable to their powers."

In pursuance of this resolution, a class was opened on Thursday, March 6th, for instruction in book-keeping; and during a term of three months it was attended, with more or less regularity, by ten pupils. The progress made by some of the number was very encouraging. In other cases there were great difficulties to contend with, arising from incomplete knowledge of arithmetic, and the angular handwriting now commonly taught in girls' schools was also found to be a serious drawback. The class was closed for the summer season on May 30th, and re-opened on Thursday, October 10th. It is hoped that some of the members of this class will be prepared to pass the Examination of the Society of Arts in 1862.*

In the month of May, a Register for Governesses was opened, under the direction of a member of the Committee, in the working of which some significant facts have been brought into notice. The great disproportion between the number of applications from governesses as compared with those from employers, and the rates of salary offered as compared with the qualifications required, combine to show how largely the supply of teachers exceeds the demand.

Much valuable information has been obtained by direct inquiry. In the early part of this year, a letter was addressed to many of the principal employers of female labour in this district, containing the following queries:—

1. How many women do you employ?

2. Are they paid by time or by the piece?

3. If by time, what are the weekly wages of those employed in each of the different departments, and what are the hours?

4. If by the piece, what are the average earnings in each department, for a day of ten working hours?

5. Are the women employed under the supervision of men or women?

* It is not generally known that the Examinations of the Society of Arts, embracing a choice of twenty-nine subjects, are open to women. Programmes containing the fullest information may be obtained gratis, on application to the Secretary of the Society of Arts, Adelphi, London, W.C.

To these questions courteous replies were received, with many kind expressions of sympathy with the work of the Society. It was ascertained that a large number of women are employed in various kinds of manual work in shops, at wages ranging from 6s. to 14s. per week. Many hundreds of women and girls are to be found in the lower and dirtier departments of the factories on the Tyne; in nursery-gardens and at field-work; some even in brick-yards. Some are paid by the day, others by the piece, but the average earnings may be roughly stated at from 4s. to 12s. per week. Except in a few special cases, these women are superintended by men. One employer writes, "I find they do better under the direction of one of themselves, with general instructions from the foreman, than under the superintendence of a man." Another states that, in his manufactory the work is given out by foremen, but done under the direction of forewomen. Probably the masters generally would be willing to employ female overseers if they could, but as it is "not the custom" to apprentice girls there are no women competent to overlook.

It is a matter of astonishment to many that girls should be found willing to work for 1s. a day, while good servants are so much in request. But the reason is not far to seek. The same difficulty meets us here as elsewhere—that of apprenticeship—for it need scarcely be pointed out that to make a good servant, a thorough apprenticeship is as much required as for other business. Every one at all acquainted with the working classes knows how eagerly any subordinate situation in "a gentleman's family" is caught up, or indeed any situation in any family where there are good opportunities of learning. But few "gentleman's families" require the services of young girls, and in smaller establishments the servant is expected to know her business before she comes. The mistresses, often unable to teach, content themselves with idly complaining that they cannot find good servants, ready made to their hands. This great difficulty at starting, no doubt, prevents many girls from becoming servants. It should also be remembered, that supposing factory girls were fit for domestic service, and inclined to enter it, the number of servants would be so enormously increased that it would be impossible to find places for them.

It has been commonly supposed that the difficulty experienced by women in finding remunerative occupation is caused by the excess of females, and that if by female emigration we could equalise the proportions of the sexes, this troublesome problem would be got rid of. Our experience of this locality does not confirm this impression. In the towns of Newcastle and Gateshead the disparity of the sexes is so slight as scarcely to affect the question. (In Newcastle the proportion is thirty nine males to forty females; in the adjoining town of Gateshead there is a slight excess of males.) No doubt, if women could be induced to emigrate in considerable numbers, the pressure would be in some degree lessened, but here, again, the apprenticeship difficulty presents itself. Untrained women are as unfit for the colonies as they are for home life. It is, indeed, no wonder that people who have not learnt to do anything cannot find anything to do. A man in a similar position would perhaps find himself even more helpless than a woman. The real cause of the difficulty lies in the unaccountable thought-lessness of parents, who seem to take a certain pride in keeping their daughters idle, and in the general dislike to innovations. While parents show them-selves indifferent, we can scarcely wonder, however much we may regret it, that master-manufacturers and tradesmen are reluctant to make the little alterations in their arrangements that would be rendered necessary by the introduction of women. In former times girls were taught, and thoroughly taught, the various branches of manufacture which were then carried on in every house. Unfortunately for the present generation we have not yet learnt to accommodate ourselves to the great change which, during the last fifty years, has been silently going forward in our domestic life. The introduction of machinery has taken out of the hands of women the spinning and the weaving, the knitting and the sewing, which once furnished them with such abun-dant and profitable occupation. There appears to be but one resource, and happily it is one from which we need not shrink. We must gradually and, in the exercise of a wise discretion, open to women, through a regular apprenticeship, all trades and pro-fessions for which they are not physically disqualified.

The employment of women

Let us not be mistaken. We do not expect or wish to turn factory-girls into clerks and cashiers, or cooks and housemaids into physicians and lawyers. We *do* wish to see factory-girls, if girls are to be in factories at all, in the departments where skill rather than strength is required, and under the supervision of women. We wish to see the poor degraded women who supply the factories with labour cheaper than that of boys gradually drawn up into the ranks of domestic servants. We wish to see the class of young women near to these in degree able to earn a sufficient income to live respectably, and to lay by something for the future. We wish to see mistresses working *with* their young servants and teaching them all the little arts which adorn and beautify our English homes. We wish to see all women who have not households to look after, engaged in some other occupation sufficiently absorbing to be the business of a life. We wish to see the *variety* of ability, which is confessedly as great in women as in men, more fully recognised; and finally, we wish and confidently expect, to see the day when idleness will be considered not ladylike, but unwomanly, and when those at least who desire to learn and to follow some honourable calling will not be debarred by the false pride of parents or the prejudices of trade.

Medicine as a profession for women.

[Read at the Annual Meeting of the National Association for the promotion of Social Science, 1862.]

In speaking of Medicine as a profession for women, it is not my intention to enter upon the general question of the employment of women. I may be allowed, however, in passing, to protest against a notion which seems to have taken possession of many minds, that those who are endeavouring to extend the range of women's labour, are desirous of adding to the severity of their toil. Women already work hard, and it ought scarcely to be said that we wish to increase the aggregate amount of their labour. What we are striving for is rather a re-adjustment of the burden, a somewhat different apportionment of mental and physical labour as relatively distributed between men and women. We desire to see such a condition of society as is described by Coleridge, who in picturing an imagined golden age, speaks of it as a time " when labour was a sweet name for the activity of sane minds in healthful bodies." It is not too much to say that the great mass of women are much less healthy, both in mind and body, than they might be if they had a fair chance of physical and mental development. Many ladies are sickly and hysterical, not, strictly speaking, from want of work, but from want of some steady occupation, sufficiently interesting and important to take them out of themselves. The very poor, on the other hand, are worn down by an amount and a kind of physical toil for which their frames were never intended, their minds being utterly uncultivated, while their earnings are so small that it is impossible for them to maintain themselves in decency and comfort.* Of neither of these classes can it be fairly said that they are in that state of life into which it has pleased God to call them. Some other agency must be at work, some disturbing cause, hindering them from filling their appropriate positions. It is to help them to find their place, and to occupy it when found, that our efforts are directed.

If it be true, as the most experienced persons tell us, that what women want in the way of employment is something which gives room for the exercise of their mental activities, without excessive physical toil, we are led to inquire in what professions and occupations these conditions can be obtained. For ladies, it is also requisite that the occupation should not involve the forfeiture of social position. A parent may reasonably say, "I feel that my daughter would be better and happier with some definite work, but what can I bring her up to?" The prac-

---

* Those who have come into immediate contact, as I have, with the female workers in glass-houses, paper-mills, brick-yards, &c., will confess that this is no exaggerated statement.

tice of Medicine among women and children, as being to all appearance essentially a woman's work, naturally occurs first, and we have now to consider whether it fulfils the before-mentioned conditions. As to the first—no one doubts that the study and practice of Medicine afford ample scope for the use of the mental powers. Some persons have indeed expressed a fear that, the minds of women being naturally inferior, the strain on their faculties would be too great. There seems little reason, however, to apprehend danger on this score, as a little observation proves that the most highly cultivated women, whose mental energies are at least as much in use as those of the average doctors, are not less healthy-minded than others, but rather the reverse. With regard to bodily exertion, there is no doubt that a physician in full practice goes through a very considerable amount of work. But after all, walking, and riding, and driving about, are among the recognised means of gaining health, and even the night work, of which some share falls to the lot of all doctors, is perhaps not much more trying to the constitution than the night work habitually performed by ladies of all ages, in heated rooms, and under other unfavourable circumstances. It should be understood throughout that in making these comparisons, I speak of the general run of doctors all over the country, not of a few picked men at the head of their profession, on whose energies the demand must be extraordinarily great, and with whom it would not be necessary for ladies to compete.

Medicine as a profession for women
1862]

The last-named condition—that the profession should not involve the sacrifice of social position—is the one which marks out Medicine as eminently suitable for women of the middle-class. We are constantly told that women are made to be nurses, and that a better class of nurses is urgently required. But it seems to be forgotten that though a few philanthropic ladies may undertake nursing in hospitals, or among the poor, as a work of charity, without loss of social rank, the business of a hired nurse cannot be looked upon as a profession for a lady. The salary of a hospital nurse is less than the wages of a butler or a groom, and even supposing that superior women would command higher remuneration, the position of a nurse is in every way too nearly allied to that of an upper servant, to be in the least appropriate for the daughters and sisters of the mercantile and professional classes.

Apart from the foregoing considerations, which apply chiefly to the want of some outlet for the mental energies of women, there is another aspect of the question, which ought not to be overlooked. I refer to the want of women in the medical profession. The existence of this want is not generally admitted by medical men, but I submit that they are not likely to be the best judges. It is an unquestionable fact—and here I speak, not from hearsay or conjecture but from personal knowledge obtained by extended inquiry—that women of all ranks, do earnestly desire the attendance of physicians of their own sex. The want is most strongly felt by those

who cannot command the services of the higher
class of medical men. It is equally unquestionable,
and here again I speak from authority, that women
wish to enter the profession. Is not the mere existence of these two corresponding facts a sufficient
reason for giving leave to try the experiment? If
we fail, we fail, and having fairly tried, we shall be
content to abide by the result. That an innovation
is an innovation, is not a sufficient ground for
opposing it. The opponents of a change are bound
to give reasons for their resistance. In the case
under consideration I am ready to admit that they
have done so freely. Some of the objections seem
indeed to cancel each other. For instance, one asks,
"Where are your lady students to come from?"
while another complains, "What is to become of the
men, if women crowd into this already overstocked
profession?" At one time women are ordered to
keep their place, while at another they are assured
that their place is at the bedside of the sick. Those
who are most anxious to see women waiting upon
male patients as nurses, consider it an outrage upon
propriety that they should attend their own sex as
physicians.

There are, however, more serious difficulties than
these thoughtless cavils. It cannot be denied that
there are grave objections to the study of medicine
by male and female students in mixed schools, and
although a few exceptional women might be willing,
for the sake of others, to go through the medical
course, even under existing arrangements, it is evident

that for female students generally, some modification of these arrangements would be necessary. Such a modification might easily be effected, if the demand for it were clearly made out. Separate classes might be formed for lady students in connexion with the existing schools. There would be no difficulty in obtaining the services of eminent medical men as teachers. Some of those who most strongly object to the admission of ladies into the schools for men, have expressed their willingness to give separate instruction. The examination must, of course, be the same for both sexes, as a security that the standard of proficiency should not be lowered for women, but to that there can be no objection. The difficulty of the case arises, neither from a want of apitude on the part of women, to whom the practice of Medicine seems to come more naturally than to men, nor from opposition of the medical authorities, many of whom have shown marked liberality and freedom from prejudice. The real obstacles are the unwillingness of young women to incur the reproach of singularity and self-sufficiency, and the less excusable unwillingness of their parents and friends to aid them in overcoming difficulties which they cannot conquer alone. The medical course ought to be begun early in life, and young women cannot be expected to force themselves into a profession against the wishes of those to whom they have learnt to look up for advice and guidance. At the same time, it should be remembered that no class are more sensitively alive to the influence of public opinion than

the parents of daughters. Many people who would
be favourable to women-physicians in the abstract,
would shrink from giving the least encouragement
to their own daughters to take a single step out of
the beaten path. And it is here that we can all do
something. We can at least refrain from joining in
the thoughtless cry of horror and astonishment at the
idea of women-physicians. Ladies may help much by
simply making known in the proper quarters their
wish for the medical attendance of women. By so
doing they would encourage ladies to offer themselves
as students, and would afford to them a moral support
which they much need. We cannot, indeed, save
them from the prominence which must be the lot of
the pioneers in any movement, a prominence which
has little attraction for those thoughtful women, who,
feeling the responsibilities of life more strongly than
others, are more earnest in desiring to take their
modest share in the work of the world. A certain
amount of notoriety is unavoidable, but it rests
with the public to decide whether it shall be an
unmerited stigma or an honourable distinction.

The influence of University Degrees on the education of women.

[*The Victoria Magazine*, 1863.]

IN considering the education of women in connexion with recent proposals for its improvement by means of examinations for University Degrees, it may be well to inquire at the outset, what *is* a Degree? In what does its value consist?

A University degree is neither more nor less than a certificate. At Oxford and Cambridge it certifies that the graduate has lived during a certain number of terms in a college or hall, has been devoting his time chiefly to study, and has passed divers examinations which were meant to test his ability and knowledge. The degrees of the University of London also certified in the beginning, that graduates in Arts and Laws had been students during two years, at one or other of the affiliated institutions, which were to the University of London what the colleges are to the Universities of Oxford and Cambridge. Few will deny the advantages of residence for two or three years in a college; and it may be easily seen how such residence, and the intercourse between students which it implies, may be made very greatly to lessen the dangers and disadvantages from which mere examination, taken alone, can scarcely be wholly free. It is possible that a young man, preparing at home for his degree, may be sufficiently crammed to pass, and may even find his name somewhere in the list of honours; and yet mistake knowledge for wisdom, and a retentive memory for genius. But in a college, such a man would be pretty sure to find his true level. He would find among his companions some, who with far less than his own powers of memory or application, would still unquestionably be his superiors. He would be made to feel quite easily, and almost without knowing how useful a lesson he was learning, that processes are almost as valuable as results; that what a man is, is of far more importance than what at any given time he can do; and that there are a thousand excellences that can find no room for display in any University examination whatever. Moreover, residence for two or three years in a college implies comparatively easy circumstances, and ought, therefore, to imply all that society expects from gentlemen; and though many of the colleges connected with the University of London required no extravagant expenditure, and were, perhaps, not half so costly as those of Oxford and Cambridge, yet the term of residence was generally longer, being in many of them as long as five years.

The University of London, however, was intended to promote the education, not only of gentlemen, and of persons who could afford to live for several years at a college, but of all classes of Her Majesty's subjects, without any distinction whatever; and accordingly in the new Charter it was provided, that persons not educated in any of the institutions connected with the University, should be admitted as candidates for matriculation, and degrees, "other than degrees in medicine or surgery, on such conditions as the Chancellor, Vice-Chancellor, and Fellows by regulations in that behalf should from time to time determine; such regulations being subject to the provisos and restrictions contained in the Charter." This change was regarded with considerable disfavour by many of those who had graduated under the old regulations, and who imagined that the value of their degrees would be reduced when similar degrees were conferred upon those who had never been to a college at all. It is obvious however, that the colleges must look for their prosperity to their own intrinsic worth; and that the University should confer degrees upon all those who could pass the examination prescribed, wherever they might have been educated, was clearly in harmony with the original intention of the University. The want of college training, and especially of the indirect advantage of association with men whose favourite studies lie in different directions, and who possess very different kinds of ability, was partly counteracted by the wide range of subjects in which candidates for degrees were required to pass. Nor has the change as yet done much more than recognise a right which it would have been invidious to withhold. Scarcely any of those who have taken honours during the last few years, have come to their examinations from "private study," and sixteen out of the twenty who have taken the degree of Bachelor of

Science are from the colleges connected with the University. But after all, if a man can read Livy or Thucydides, Plato's Republic, or Aristotle's Ethics, it really matters little how he obtained his knowledge of Greek and Latin ; and if it be expedient to found a University at all, and if degrees are of any use, then the man who can prove that he possesses the requisite knowledge, has a fair claim to have that fact certified.

But if the want of money, and, what amounts to very much the same thing, the want of leisure, are to be no impediment to the recognition of a man's real worth and attainments, so far as examination can test them, why should any impediments whatever be allowed to remain ? Why especially should difference of sex be an impediment ?

The question was raised so early as 1856, in which year a lady applied for admission to the examinations of the University of London. The advice of counsel was taken, and an opinion was given that such admission could not legally be granted. No further steps were taken until April, 1862, when another lady preferred a request to be admitted as a candidate at the next Matriculation Examination. On that occasion a resolution was passed : " That the Senate, as at present advised, sees no reason to doubt the validity of the opinion given by Mr. Tomlinson, July 9th, 1856, as to the admissibility of females to the Examinations of the University." The matter was not allowed to rest here. On April 30th the following memorial was laid before the Senate.

Women and University Degrees

"Gentlemen,—An application having been made by my daughter for admission to the Examinations of your University, and refused on legal grounds, we beg respectfully to request that the question may receive further consideration.

"It appears to us very desirable to raise the standard of female education, and that this object can in no way be more effectually furthered than by affording to women an opportunity of testing their attainments in the more solid branches of learning. It is usually admitted that examinations are almost essential as a touchstone of successful study, and as a stimulus to continuous effort. Such a touchstone, and such a stimulus, are even more necessary to women than to men; and though we should be most unwilling to obtain these advantages by the sacrifice of others still more precious, we are of opinion that in the University of London our object might be obtained without any contingent risk. Many of the candidates for degrees would probably be furnished by the existing Ladies' Colleges, and as the University requires no residence, and the examinations involve nothing which could in the slightest degree infringe upon feminine reserve, we believe that by acceding to our wishes you would be conferring an unmixed benefit.

"We are informed that a new Charter of the University is about to be submitted to Parliament. We beg therefore to suggest that the technical legal objection, which appears to be the only obstacle to the admission of women, may be removed by the insertion of a clause expressly providing for the extension to women of the privileges of the University. I beg to enclose a list of ladies and gentlemen who have given their sanction to the proposal.

"I have the honour to be, Gentlemen,

"Your obedient Servant,

"NEWSON GARRETT."

On May 7th a resolution was moved by the Vice-Chancellor, Mr. Grote, and seconded by the Right Hon. R. Lowe, M.P., to the effect, "That the Senate will endeavour, as far as their powers reach, to obtain a modification of the Charter, rendering female students admissible to the Degrees and Honours of the University of London, on the same conditions of examination as male students, but not rendering them admissible to become Members of Convocation." After an earnest and protracted discussion, the Senate divided. The numbers being equal, ten on each side, the motion was negatived by the casting vote of the Chancellor. The following reply to the Memorial was addressed to Mr. Garrett.

"Sir,—I am directed to inform you that, after a full consideration of your Memorial, the Senate have come to the conclusion that it is not expedient to propose any alteration in the Charter, with a view of obtaining power to admit females to the Examinations of the University.

"I think it well to add, that this decision has not been the result of any indisposition to give encouragement to the higher education of the female sex—a very general concurrence having been expressed in the desire stated in your Memorial, that an opportunity should be afforded to women of testing their attainments in the more solid branches of learning; but it has been based on the conviction entertained by the majority of the Senate, that it is not desirable that the constitution of this University should be modified for the sake of affording such opportunity.

> " I remain, Sir,
> " Your obedient Servant,
> " W. B. CARPENTER."

The matter has since been brought forward in the Convocation of the University. On the 26th March a Resolution was passed by the Annual Committee, and afterwards embodied in the Report to Convocation, to the following effect: " That this Committee, recognising the desirableness of elevating the standard of female education, recommend Convocation to represent to the Senate the propriety of considering whether it might not forward the objects of the University, as declared in the Charter, to make provision for the examination and certification of women." After a lengthened discussion the resolution was negatived by a considerable majority.

The question having thus been fairly raised—a definite application having been made—it clearly becomes the duty of those who decline to accede to a request which appears so reasonable, to show cause for their refusal. The *onus probandi* undoubtedly rests with the opponents of the measure. And it must be confessed that they have not been backward in accepting the challenge, whatever may be thought of the quality of the arguments brought forward. They resolve themselves, for the most part, into an "instinct," a prejudice, or an unproved assertion that women ought not to pursue the same studies as men; and that they would become exceedingly unwomanly if they did. A woman so educated would, we are assured, make a very poor wife or mother. Much learning would make her mad, and would wholly unfit her for those quiet domestic offices for which Providence intended her. She would lose the gentleness, the grace, and the sweet vivacity which are now her chief adornment, and would become cold, calculating, masculine, fast, strongminded, and in a word, generally unpleasing. That the evils described under these somewhat vague terms are very real, and do actually exist at this moment, cannot be denied by any one who is at all conversant with English society. That any scheme of education which might tend to foster them, ought to be energetically resisted, will scarcely be disputed by any—least of all by the advocates of extended mental culture for women.

It may be well to examine first, that theory of the difference between manhood and womanhood which underlies most of the objections commonly brought against the thorough culture of women; and which, if it were true, would render all further argument superfluous. The differences between a man and a woman are either essential or conventional, or both. In any case it is difficult to understand how they

affect the right of a woman to pass an examination
and to take a degree. The differences themselves are
often exaggerated, both by women and by men. So
far as they are manifested by any external acts, they
are almost entirely conventional; and of those which
are essential, and which belong to the inmost being
of woman or man, it seems difficult to understand
how any information can be obtained, or comparison
instituted. For how can things be compared which
ex-hypothesi are wholly unlike? How can we
possibly know or learn that to which there is nothing
analogous in ourselves? We understand the nature
of animals because, and in so far as, we are animals
ourselves. To the same extent possibly a dog might
understand a man; but no ingenuity could ever
impart to an animal the knowledge of the human
spirit, with all its endless resources, its freedom, its
aspirations, its power to "look before and after."
Nothing could make a brute religious, or explain to
a brute what religion is; and, on the other side, are
we not taught that we can know God only so far as
we are partakers of the Divine nature; only because
God created man in His own image? If there be
then in woman a mystic something to which nothing
in a man corresponds; if woman has what man
wants, or wants what man has; if this difference be
natural, essential, and therefore for ever unalterable,
it simply marks out a region of utter unlikeness
which is protected by that unlikeness from intrusion
or visitation. Perhaps then we may leave altogether
out of the question those mystic differences which

can give no clear proof of their own existence, which have no faculty of speech, no means of expressing what they are.

But at any rate, there are differences, we are told, which can manifest themselves. The strength of the woman, we are told, is in the heart; the strength of the man, in the head. The woman can suffer patiently; the man can act bravely. The woman has a loving care for the individual; the man an unimpassioned reverence for the general and universal. These, and such as these, are represented as the outward tokens of essential differences, which cannot be mistaken, and ought never, in any system of education or work of life, to be overlooked.

If these are natural differences, it is idle to ask whether we should praise or blame them, for the nature of a thing has no moral qualities whatever. A tiger may be dangerous, but is certainly not cruel; a fox may be cunning, but cannot be dishonest; and if dogs delight to bark and bite, because God hath made them so, who shall find fault with them? But natural differences should certainly guide our systems of education; and if it is really in the nature of a woman to have very much feeling and very little sense, were it not a kind of fighting against Providence to attempt to rescue her from this very dangerous form of insanity? Yet, surely, it may be affirmed with the utmost confidence, that a woman's affections ought to be as well regulated as a man's; that she should know how to give as well as to receive, and be prompt to act as well as patient to suffer. She should not sacrifice the many for the one, nor the long endless future for the passing moment. And do we really wish to people the world with male creatures devoid of all gentleness and affection, losing sight of the individual in the mass, irritable and impatient under the irremediable discomforts and reverses of life? Does religion include no tender affections for the man, no intellectual strength for the woman? And do we not read that God created man in His own image, in the image of God created He him, male and female created He them? Should not a man's thoughts of God be a woman's thoughts also? And why should that compassion of the Almighty, which is spoken of in Scripture as womanly, be strange to the heart of man? A woman surely ought to have a sense of the law of justice, and a man, of the law of love. Moreover, a genius for detail is quite worthless if the parts are not fittingly arranged and subordinated to the whole.

In truth, it is exactly in this subordinating of the whole to its parts that even the charity and affection of women has often done great mischief; and is capable of doing any amount of mischief, if it were not restrained by that power of generalisation and order which now women sometimes find in men, and ought to find in themselves. A beggar dying in the streets of starvation should be relieved by anybody who is able to relieve him; his individual life is not to be sacrificed for any theory or system, however comprehensive. If it is a man who sees him perishing with want he would be bound, and we may fairly hope he would be willing, to save him. On the other hand, the majority of street-beggars are impostors, and certainly ought not to be relieved. To relieve them is a direct encouragement of idleness and vice. Even the little children, who will certainly be cruelly flogged unless they take home a fair amount of money after a day's suffering and shame, would never be employed in so shameful a business as begging if ill-regulated kindness had not made it profitable. Individually they may be as greatly in need of assistance as any sufferers whatever; the reasons why they are not to receive alms are reasons derived from the careful combination and comparison of very many facts of very different kinds. Is it really thought desirable, then, that women should be ignorant of those facts, and the general rules deduced from them? Is the wisdom of the male sex to be for ever fighting against the tender-heartedness of the female sex? And is the thought of man to form wise and useful rules of conduct, only that the impulsiveness of woman may break them? But why do women look to the individual rather than to the many, and deal with separate examples rather than with general rules? It is surely not necessary to look for any recondite and essential ground of this difference if we can find one obvious and conventional, which will account equally well for the phenomenon. Women, in fact, have never been instructed in general principles. A man talks to a man about the statistics of poverty or crime; they carefully consider together what are the causes which, in the majority of cases, have produced either of these gigantic evils; causes, such as ignorance, drunkenness and the like. They do their best, therefore, not to collect money to give away in alms to any beggar who may ask their assistance, but they establish a school, provide places of refreshment and amusement, orderly and well-conducted, and where, by satisfying natural desires, the temptation to unnatural excesses may be reduced to a minimum. They take care, or at least they know that they *ought* to take care, that the relief of poverty shall be of a kind to remove as far as possible the causes of poverty, and every new experiment they make for the relief of misery and the prevention of crime, widens their theories and improves their rules of practice. But it has not been the habit of men to talk with women, and act with them, after this manner. Without a word of instruction about the reasons for what they are about to do, they are asked to visit some poor man's cottage, and administer what relief they may think necessary; or to visit some school or workhouse, or to collect money, or to make clothes, like Dorcas. It is surely not very surprising that women confine themselves to that sort of work which alone has been entrusted to them from generation to generation. It is not wonderful that they do that sort of work well, nor does it require any mystic difference between the sexes to account for the fact that they do not know what, through hundreds of generations, they have neither been required nor encouraged to learn.

We are told, however, that the course of study required for obtaining a degree in the University of London is altogether unfit for women. "Do the advocates of the Burlington House degrees know," asks a writer on female education, "what is actually required by the London University for ordinary graduates? Why, the candidate is required to pass in nearly the whole range of pure arithmetical science—in geometry, plane and solid; in simple and quadratic equations; in the elements of plane trigonometry; in elementary Latin; in the history of Rome to the death of Augustus; in English composition, and English history to the end of the seventeenth century; in either French or German; in statics and dynamics treated with elementary mathematics; in an experimental knowledge of physics and optics, and a general conception of plane astronomy; in animal physiology; in elementary Greek, and Greek history up to the death of Alexander; and in the elements of logic and moral philosophy. Does any one in his (or her) senses suppose that the understanding of average young ladies would be the better for passing this examination well, or for trying to pass it anyhow, as the proper aim of their education? We might get one or two clever women, several Miss Cornelia Blimbers, and many Miss Tootses—if we may suggest an intellectual sister to Mr. Toots—out of such a system, but certainly not an improved standard for ordinary women. I believe that we should have half the young women in the country in brain fever or a lunatic asylum, if they were to make up their minds to try for it."

It is perhaps equally probable that we should have half the young *men* in the country in brain fever or a lunatic asylum, if they were to make up *their* minds to try for it. Graduates are a very small minority of the men of England, and yet their education has determined the education of the great majority who are not graduates. It is by no means obvious that it would do women any harm to know enough for the B.A. (London) pass-examination. They are already expected to learn not much less at Queen's College, in Harley Street; and a degree would be to women, in their present stage of cultivation, what honours are to men.

Women are expected to learn *something* of arithmetical science, and who shall say at what point they are to stop? Why should simple equations brighten their intellects, and quadratic equations drive them into a lunatic asylum? Why should they be the better for the three books of Euclid, which they are required to master at Queen's College, and "stupefied" by conic sections or trigonometry? Why should Latin give them a deeper insight into the philosophy of language, and introduce them to a literature and history which may raise them above the narrowness or the extravagance of their own age, and the language of the New Testament be forbidden, as too exhausting a labour, a toil fruitful only of imbecility or death? Is it really necessary that women should be shut out from the knowledge of the physical sciences? Would a knowledge of physiology make them worse mothers, and an acquaintance with the chemistry of food less fit to superintend the processes of cooking? It is not asked, be it remembered, that one single woman should be compelled to take a degree, or held disgraced for being without one; but simply, that she may try if she chooses, and that if she chooses and succeeds, then she shall receive that certificate of her strength and culture which will be fairly her due.

But the value of degrees in female education would be far greater indirectly than directly; they would raise the standard of excellence by a sure process, even though it might be slow, of every school and every teacher in the kingdom. A very small proportion of girls would attempt to take them; fewer still would succeed; fewer still would take honours. But every school-girl in the land would very soon become aware of the fact, that women might hope and strive for a thorough culture which has never yet been generally offered to them. The Arts regulations of the University of London would guide the studies of women as gently and effectually as they now guide the studies of boys and men. A very simple example of this may be given. There is an increasing neglect of the Greek and Latin Classics in ordinary education. The reason why these languages are still taught in the majority of middle-class schools is neither more nor less than this: that some knowledge of them is required for

the B.A. degree, and even for matriculation in the
University of London. That which in the case of
boys seems drawing near to death, is, in the case of
girls, just beginning to live; and the classic languages in girls' schools and colleges have to force their
way to general acceptance through many difficulties
and prejudices. The same influence which arrests
the decay in one case would favour the growth in
the other case. Whether the reasons for the study
of the classical languages be understood or not,
reasons of the utmost cogency do actually exist.
They have been considered and reconsidered over
and over again, and in all variety of circumstances,
by those who are best qualified to judge; and they
still retain their place of highest honour and prime
necessity in thorough human culture. The study
of them justifies itself in every case where they are
really studied, and not simply acquired as accomplishments. It would be a very great advantage,
and especially in a country so devoted to commerce
as our own, that they should be studied, even though
very few might perceive the reasons why. That
they were necessary for a certificate of merit, or for
a University degree, would be a satisfactory answer
for teachers to give to that large class of parents who
really know nothing about genuine education, but
who feel that they must obtain for their children
what other children have, and a reputation for knowledge at any rate, if not knowledge itself.

In the foregoing observations it is not intended to
assert that the curriculum of the London University

is absolutely the best that could possibly be devised for women. There are differences of opinion as to whether it is absolutely the best that could be devised for men. But in the meantime, here it is, ready made to our hands. Men accept it, admitting it to be imperfect, as the best at present attainable. Women are desirous of sharing its advantages and disadvantages. They need, even more than men, "an encouragement for pursuing a regular and liberal course of education" *after* the period at which their school education ceases. To found a separate University for them would be a work of enormous difficulty and expense, and one which the existence of the University of London renders unnecessary. If indeed there were no University having the power to examine and confer degrees without collegiate residence, a new institution would undoubtedly be required. As it happens, however, that quite irrespective of the claims of women, the constitution of the University of London has already been so modified as exactly to meet their requirements, the suggestion to found a new University may be regarded as simply a device for getting rid of the question.

Those who entertain the fear that an enlarged course of study would, by overworking the female brain, eventually produce wide-spread idiocy, should remember that mental disease is produced by want of occupation as well as by an excess of it. It has been stated to us by a physician at the head of a large lunatic asylum near London, having under his charge a considerable number of female patients of the middle-class, that the majority of these cases were the result of mental idleness. It is a well-known fact that in those most melancholy diseases known by the names of hysteria, and nervous affections, under which so large a proportion of women in the well-to-do classes are, more or less, sufferers, the first remedy almost invariably prescribed is, interesting occupation, change of scene, anything, in fact, that may divert the mind from the dull mono- of a vacant life.

The strongest arguments which can be used in favour of offering some stimulus to the higher intellectual culture of women are in fact those which have been thoughtlessly advanced on the other side. Amazons have never been persons of high intellectual attainments, nor have the most learned women shown any tendency to rush into Bloomerism and other ugly eccentricities. It is true, indeed, and a fact of the utmost significance, that women with great natural force of character, do, when denied a healthy outlet for their energy, often indulge in unhealthy extravagances, simply because it is a necessity of their nature to be active in some way or other. But the fast women and the masculine women are not those who sit down to their books and devote themselves to an orderly course of study. It may be asserted with still greater emphasis, that the hard and cold women are precisely those whom a consciousness of their unimportance to the world in general has made callous to everything but their own petty, personal interests, and in whom the sense of duty and responsibility, or, in other words, the conscience, has been deadened and seared by fashionable frivolity.

Great stress has been laid on the alleged fact that women do not themselves want University examinations and degrees. It is always difficult to ascertain the "sense" of women on any given subject. Many shrink from even affixing their names to a memorial, and there is no other recognised method by which they can, in any corporate manner, express their opinions. There can be no doubt that among the more thoughtful, there are many who are eager to obtain for younger women educational aids of which they cannot themselves enjoy the benefit. The cordial support given to this proposal by Mrs. Somerville, Mrs. Grote, Mrs. Gaskell, Mrs. Mary Howitt, &c., and by a large proportion of the ladies concerned in the management of Queen's College and Bedford College, sufficiently attest the fact.

It is probably equally true that there are many others who are not very anxious for any alteration in existing systems of education. This ought not to be surprising to a reflecting mind. It is perfectly natural that people who do not know by experience the value of learning, and who are pretty well satisfied with themselves as they are, should not care much about securing to others advantages which they are incapable of appreciating. The tendency, almost the professed object, of their education has been to make them unreasonable. It would be strange indeed, if on this one subject they should be able to reason and judge. *Their* indifference is much less astonishing than that of men, who willingly forego for their daughters opportunities of intellectual advancement which they well know how to appreciate, and which they consider of the highest importance for their sons.

There is one part of this subject which is of special practical importance, and also of peculiar difficulty: the right of women to take degrees in Medicine. This, it should be remembered, is wholly distinct from the general question which it has been the object of this paper to discuss. The course of study and of practice necessary for the M.B. or M.D. degree, is by no means a necessary part of that human culture which every man and every woman should be encouraged and urged to seek. But the right to practise as a physician would be valuable as opening the way for useful and remunerative employment to those ladies who do not wish to be governesses, or to engage in ordinary trade; and as affording to all women the alternative of being attended by physicians of their own sex. It cannot be denied that a large number of women find very great satisfaction in some kind or other of doctoring, and do actually practise it, whether they know anything about it or not; yet this is so grave a matter that it has been thought necessary, quite recently, to bring the practice of medicine more completely under legal control. The want of skill or care may so easily and quickly produce fatal mischief, and even murder itself may be so easily hidden under the disguise of the unskilfulness of a physician, that it has been thought necessary to require the surest guarantees of competency from all those to whose professional attention, the health and lives of their patients are so often entrusted. Here, however, as in Arts, what has been asked on the part of women is not a lower standard of medical skill, not easier examinations, but that they should be allowed, in medical schools of their own, to acquire such knowledge as would enable them to pass the examinations and acquire the skill which are now thought necessary and sufficient in the case of men.

The holding of degrees by women is not without precedent. In the Italian Universities, and in that of Göttingen, women have held high positions. Towards the end of the last century a female physician graduated at Montpelier. In 1861, the degree of *Bachelier ès-Lettres* was conferred on Mdlle. Daubié by the Academy of Lyons, and within the last few months another French lady, Mdlle. Chenu, passed her examination for the degree of *Bachelier ès-Sciences* at the University of the Sorbonne. It appears not unreasonable to hope that before many years have elapsed, Englishwomen will be placed in a not less favourable position than their continental neighbours, and that whatever advantages may belong to University examinations and degrees will be thrown freely open to them.

On Secondary Instruction as relating to girls.

[*Read at the Annual Meeting of the National Association for the promotion of Social Science, 1864.*]

IN the great controversy which, having been begun
by the debates on the Report of the Public Schools'
Commission, is now extending itself over almost the
whole department of secondary instruction, there
is an omission which seems to call for remark.
Throughout the discussion, voluminous as it has
been, the question has hitherto been treated exclusively in reference to boys, it having been tacitly
assumed that male education only is a matter of
concern to the general community. This feature
is the more remarkable, inasmuch as it is peculiar
to the present agitation. In the effort made some
years ago for the improvement of primary education,
ignorant boys and ignorant girls were recognized as
having similar needs and similar claims. National
and British Schools for girls are inspected, mistresses
are trained, female pupil-teachers are apprenticed,
and speaking generally, the education of the daughters of the labouring classes is as carefully watched
over as that of their sons. Why is the case altered
when we advance a few steps higher in the social
scale? With regard to the Public Schools, the
reason is obvious enough. As there are no Etons
for girls in existence, they could not be made the
subject of investigation. Probably the sisters of

Questions relating to Women

Public School boys are for the most part taught by governesses at home. Their education is therefore clearly beyond the scope of a Commission of Inquiry, and though it does not follow that it is a matter in which the nation has no interest, it is natural enough that it should not appear in the discussion called forth by the Commissioners' Report. But this consideration does not apply to the daughters of the middle-class, and it is difficult to understand why their early training should be regarded as a matter of less importance than that of their brothers. That it is so regarded appears to be implied by the almost total silence of the thinkers and writers to whom the nation looks for guidance. It is needless to bring proofs of what no one will deny. It is a simple fact, that in the mass of speeches, articles, reviews, pamphlets and volumes which have lately been before the public on the subject of secondary instruction for boys, there is scarcely so much as a passing allusion to that of girls. This side of the question has been, by general consent, completely ignored.

There is no reason for attributing this silence to ungenerous motives. It no doubt arises in a great degree from a sort of inadvertence. Public writers are occupied with the busy world around them, in which men only are to be seen, and it is perhaps not much to be wondered at, if they think only of training the boys, who are hereafter to do the more conspicuous part of the world's work. Some, and those the men most worth listening to, are unwilling to speak of what they imperfectly know, and it is difficult for them to know much about girls or women. When they speak of boys, they have at any rate their own experience to go upon, and it is not unnatural that they should by preference confine themselves to that side of the subject of which they have personal cognisance. Others are no doubt insensibly influenced by the view of education which regards it merely as a means of making a living. It has been remarked that "a great part of the confusion in which the question of education is involved, arises from the division of public feeling as to the value of knowledge." There are many persons who value it only as a weapon to be used in the struggle for material existence, and as women are, theoretically, never required to fight, it may seem superfluous to supply them with arms.

Women, on their part, are largely responsible for the general carelessness. It could scarcely be expected that they should very keenly appreciate advantages of which they have had no experience, and they are generally ready enough to profess themselves perfectly satisfied with things as they are, and to echo doubts as to whether "so much education is necessary for girls." Some, who are conscious of their own deficiencies, are afraid that the manifestation of a desire to help others may be mistaken for an assumption of great enlightenment in themselves. Others, who by unusual energy and perseverance have succeeded in gaining knowledge, and the power that it brings with it, are, by their very superiority, cut off from the multitude. They look down from their heights, with little sympathy, on the mass of women tamely giving way before difficulties which they have known how to overcome. Others again shrink from prominence in any cause whatever; their dread of publicity is so overpowering that they would rather see a whole generation drowning before their eyes in ignorance and sloth, than run the slightest risk of being spoken of as having taken part in the rescue. I should be sorry to speak of this reserve with anything like disrespect; I believe it is seldom absent from the finest natures. But I submit that it is one of the duties imposed upon women of this generation to speak out, careless of the cost, on those questions of which they can most fitly judge. Silence and inaction are not justified by any of the reasons here suggested; for whatever may be the causes—or the excuses—the result is the same. The impression is conveyed to the public mind that the education of girls is an affair of very little consequence—that it is, in fact, one of the things which may safely and properly be left to take care of themselves. It is no wonder that so agreeable an untruth should meet with ready acceptance.

In venturing to raise a protest against both the doctrine itself, and the policy which it involves, I do not propose to enter upon an inquiry into the condition of girls' schools, and the systems of teaching pursued. It is one of the results of the prevailing indifference, that nobody knows enough of the interior of girls' schools to speak with authority about them. The data for forming a general conclusion are not within the reach of any individual. But there is a method by which we may test the quality of the schools:—we can look at the quality of the thing produced. Anybody, or at least any woman, may know what girls are after leaving school, and we may fairly judge of the process by its results, making allowance, of course, for extenuating circumstances in the shape of vitiating home influences.*

I ask then, what are girls worth when their education is finished? What are they good for? Are they in vigorous health of mind or body? What is there that they care about? How are their lives filled up? What have they to talk about? What do they read? I am speaking, let it be remembered, not of children, but of grown-up women. Does anybody care for their opinions on any but the most trivial matters? Have they a thought beyond the circle of petty cares?

To all these questions favourable answers might be returned as regards many exceptional women. But if we look at the great mass, we shall find much to be ashamed of. On all sides there is evidence that as regards intelligence and good sense, English women of the middle class are held in small esteem. "A woman's reason" means, in popular phrase, no reason at all. A man who lets it be known that he

---

* In fairness to the schools it ought perhaps to be remarked that they are moulded by public opinion. Many schoolmistresses supply what society demands, very much against their own judgment and inclination.

consults his wife, endangers his own reputation for sense. A habit of exaggeration, closely verging upon untruthfulness, is a recognised feminine characteristic. Newspaper writers, expressing the prevailing sentiment, assume towards women an indulgent air which is far from flattering, giving them credit for plenty of good intentions, but very little capacity; and the tone in which many ladies speak of the capabilities of women is still more depreciatory than that adopted by men. No doubt this is partly exaggerated and unjust. All *classes,* as such, are now and then maligned, and so long as women are unfortunately regarded as a class, they will come in for their share of ridicule. But without taking the current raillery too much *au sérieux,* it will be admitted that the popular estimate of a woman's mental worth is somewhat low.

This condition of mental weakness might not be looked upon as so very grave a misfortune, if it was made up for by bodily strength. We are learning more and more the importance of physical health to the life of a nation, and a training which should produce a thoroughly sound physique, even at the expense of feebleness of mind, would have much to recommend it. But women are not healthy. It is a rare thing to meet with a lady, of any age, who does not suffer from headaches, langour, hysteria, or some ailment showing a want of stamina. Shut out, in towns especially, from wholesome sources of excitement, they either resort to such as are unwholesome, or else fall into indolent habits, losing strength from

want of exercise, and constantly requiring change of
air and scene as a substitute for the healthy stimulus
of regular exertion. Dulness is not healthy, and the
lives of ladies are, it must be confessed, exceedingly
dull. Men recall pictures of homely households in
earlier times, and imagine that such things are, or
might be, going on still. They forget the prosaic
fact, that the continually increasing use of all sorts of
machinery for the supply of household wants has
completely altered the aspect of our domestic interiors.
The rounded life of our grandmothers, full of interest
and variety and usefulness, is a thing of the past.
Some of us may look back upon it with regret, but
it can never be recalled. How can women, living
in towns where they can buy almost every article in
domestic use cheaper than they could make it, unless
they reckon their time and eyesight as worth nothing
at all, work with spirit at tasks which are obviously
futile? It is not in human nature. It is not in
women's nature even, mysteriously inconsequent as
that nature is believed to be. I may seem to be
wandering from the point, but it will be seen, I hope,
that if the old avocations, involving abundant exercise of all the faculties, are being taken away, it
becomes necessary to supply their place by new
interests and occupations. A hundred years ago,
women might know little of history and geography,
and nothing at all of any language but their own—
they might be careless of what was going on in the
outer world—ignorant of science and art—but their
minds were not therefore necessarily inactive. Cir-

cumstances provided a discipline which is now wholly wanting, and which needs to be supplied by wider and deeper cultivation. I dwell upon this point because I am sure that busy people, and especially busy men, have a very faint and feeble conception of what dulness is. They overtax their own brains, and by way of compensation, they have invented the doctrine of vicarious rest, according to which, men are justified in wearing themselves out so long as women can be kept in a state of wholesome rust. We hear a great deal of the disastrous effects which would follow if women were to abandon the habits of elegant leisure by which the balance is supposed to be redressed. The *otium* SINE *dignitate* of drawing-rooms presents itself to men's minds in enviable contrast with the bustle and turmoil of an active career. They

"Hearken what the inner spirit sings;
There is no joy but calm."

And they think dulness is calm. If they had ever tried what it is to be a young lady, they would know better.

The system tells in different ways, according to the individual character. Some girls fret and pine under it; others, satisfying their souls with husks, are content to idle about from morning till night, acquiring, as has been already said, indolent and desultory habits, hard to break through when in later life the demand for steady, methodical exertion comes upon them. Some take to works of charity, doing some harm, and no doubt also some good Their usefulness is at any rate seriously lessened by the want of the cultivated judgment to guide and control benevolent impulse. Some, I gladly admit, lead noble lives, filling their leisure with worthy pursuits, and in spite of difficulties, tracing out for themselves a useful and happy career.

It may seem to be entering upon somewhat low ground to speak of women's talk, but it may not be out of place, seeing that, as things are, it forms a chief part of their business. And what do ladies talk about at morning calls and evening parties? Children, servants, dress and summer tours—all very good subjects in themselves, but so treated, partly through sheer ignorance, that as conversation advances, tedium grows, till at last all signs of intelligence disappear, and the weary countenances too faithfully reveal the vacancy within. Of literature, women of the middle class know next to nothing. I am not speaking of religious literature, which is extensively read by some women, and to which they owe much. I speak of general literature, and of ordinary women, whose reading is for the most part confined to novels, and of novels not the best. The catalogue of a bookseller's circulating library, in which second-rate fiction largely preponderates, is a fair criterion of the range and the taste of middle class lady readers. Newspapers are scarcely supposed to be read by women at all. When the *Times* is offered to a lady, the sheet containing the advertisements, and the Births, Deaths, and Marriages, is considerately selected.

This almost complete mental blankness being the ordinary condition of women, it is not to be wondered at that their opinions, when they happen to have any, are not much respected. In those cases indeed, where natural sagacity is a sufficient guide, women often form just conclusions, but manifestly, wherever knowledge of facts is required, they are almost sure to be at fault. And very few questions of any importance can be decided without such knowledge. Of what is going on in the world women know little and care less. When political or social questions are forced upon their notice they commonly judge them from some purely personal point of view. Right and wrong are elements which scarcely enter into the calculation.

In taking this melancholy view of the middle class female mind, I am aware that I lay myself open to the attacks of two classes of objectors. By one class the picture will be condemned as a caricature, by the other it will be accepted as faithful; but it will be maintained that the defects pointed out are traceable, not to want of education, but to the natural inferiority of the female intellect. To the first I can only reply that I speak from personal knowledge supported by the experience of other observers, and, that, for all that has been said, I could, if space permitted, adduce abundant evidence. The second objection is not easy to meet, in the paucity of material for proof on either side. I believe I may say, however, on behalf of the advocates of female education, that any objector is welcome to assert anything he likes about the inferiority of the female intellect, if only he does not rate it so low as to be incapable of improvement by cultivation. We are not encumbered by theories about equality or inequality of mental power in the sexes. All we claim is that the intelligence of women, be it great or small, shall have full and free development. And we claim it not specially in the interest of women, but as essential to the growth of the human race. This is not the place to discuss whether women have, or ought to have, any other than merely domestic relations. I take the commonly received theory that except as wives, mothers, daughters, or sisters, women have no *raison d'être* at all; and on this neutral ground I urge the impolicy of neglecting female education. For now, more than ever before, the mutual influence of the sexes makes it impossible to serve one without the other. Of this fact, often enough asserted in theory, though little regarded in practice, the revelations of the Royal Commission have furnished a new and striking demonstration. In one of the recent debates it was pointed out by Mr. Gladstone that the idleness and ignorance of Public School boys are largely attributable to the over-indulgent atmosphere of the homes in which they are brought up, and the Commissioners' Report contains repeated testimonies to the same effect. Mr. Matthew Arnold says of our highest class that its culture has declined. Young men at the Universities exhibit " a slackness," " a sleep of the mind," which he traces to " a torpor of intellectual life, a dearth of idea, an indifference to fine culture or disbelief in its necessity, spreading through the bulk of our highest class and influencing its rising generation. . . . . . Never," he says, "in all its history, has our whole highest class shown such zeal for enjoying life, for amusing itself." Is this surprising? Is it not precisely what might have been expected in a society which, for at least one generation, has been content to bring up its girls to be mere elegant triflers? Is it not true, that to amuse themselves and other people is the great object in the life of women of the non-working classes, and is it possible that their sedulous devotion to this one object can fail to react upon the men with whom they associate? Who gives the tone to the lax and luxurious homes of the wealthy? Who teaches the boys that hard work is foolish self-torture, that an easy life is more to be desired than the fine gold of intellectual attainment? Not their fathers, for though they too may be led away by the prevailing passion for play, they have had a nobler ideal set before them. What is the ideal presented to a young girl? Is it anything higher than to be amiable, inoffensive, always ready to give pleasure and to be pleased? Could anything be more stupefying than such a conception of the purposes of existence? And is it likely that, constituted as society now is, young men will escape the snare which has been spread for their sisters?

In a lower social grade, the temptations assume a more sordid character. We get the trifling without the elegance. Mr. Arnold has told us in the most eloquent and convincing language, what the middle class wants. Its virtues and its defects, what it has and what it needs, have been held up to view, and those whose knowledge of that great class is most intimate will most promptly recognise the admirable faithfulness of the portrait. We are told that it is "traversed by a strong intellectual ferment,"—that it has "real mental ardour, real curiosity." Whether it will attain to "a high commanding pitch of culture and intelligence," depends on "the sensibility which it has for perfection, on its power to *transform itself.*" And "in its public action this class has hitherto shown only the power and disposition to *affirm itself*, not at all the power and disposition to *transform itself.*" Here again, we are reaping what our fathers have sown. A young man of the middle class, who enters upon life with generous instincts and aspirations after perfection, is apt gradually to lose them. He becomes day by day less public-spirited, more engrossed by selfish aims. The more home-loving he is, the more likely is this to be the case. In his best moments, where is he to look for sympathy? His highest thoughts and feelings cannot be shared by those nearest and dearest to him. Any expression of them is likely to be met by a blank, uncomprehending stare. If there is any question of a small sacrifice to be made for the good of his town or parish, he is advised against it. That his first duty is to think of his children, or, in other words, always to make the aggrandisement of his own family his primary consideration, is a maxim about which his wife feels not the slightest doubt, and which she never fails to impress upon him. In the home circle the conversation is inevitably restricted to petty subjects. The master of the house may discourse upon politics, or literature, or any other topic that may happen to interest him, but there can be no intelligent response, no interchange of thought, no pleasant discussion of things worth talking about. He may lay down the law on matters of which he knows nothing whatever, betraying the grossest ignorance of elementary facts, in full confidence that his conclusions, whether true or false, will be accepted with equal indifference. He will learn unconsciously, but very surely, that the great thing for him to do is to stick to his business, think of nothing else, talk of nothing else, aspire after nothing else. Making money and getting on in the world by means of it, are things that his wife, and his mother, and his daughters can understand and care for. They know all about the advantages of having a carriage and servants, and " a position," and plenty of money to do what they like with. If he wants to please them, the way is plain. It may not be the way he would have chosen. He may have had unselfish impulses, some "aptitude for ideas," some longings after a nobler career. But a fire which for fuel is perpetually fed with cold water soon dies out. The man who was teachable, impressible, *growing*—hardens into the mere man of business, worldly-minded, narrow-hearted, self-satisfied. I do not mean this statement to be taken in a universal sense. Of course it is sometimes the other way. The wife is

Secondary Instruction

cultivated and aspiring, and the husband drags her down. But I believe I have given a tolerably accurate account of the *tendencies* in the great mass of English homes of the middle class.

Why should this unsatisfactory state of things be allowed to continue? Why should not our English homes be animated by a spirit of truth and of sacrifice—pervaded by an atmosphere of light and warmth, in which all high thoughts and generous impulses should live and grow, all mean and selfish ends be, by common consent, disowned and utterly renounced? Why might not the family circle be a place where "example teacheth, company comforteth, emulation quickeneth"—our daily domestic intercourse like iron sharpening iron, mutually kindling, and stimulating to noble thoughts and deeds? What a change would then come over the whole aspect of our national life! What problems would be solved, what terrible enigmas disappear! How little need should we then have of philanthropic schemes for elevating the poor! How naturally would they share in all social reforms, how inevitably would they be refined and civilised by the insensible influence—the best of all influences—of the employing class, whose ideas, unconsciously communicated to their subordinates, gradually leaven all the classes below them. Masters and mistresses reveal in their everyday life in what their ideal of blessedness consists, and that ideal becomes, with some modifications, that of the humbler homes of working men and women. I say with modifications, because working *men* are through their mutual association subject to counteracting influences, and it is chiefly in so far as that of wives and mothers prevails over others scarcely less strong, that the ideas of the employing class penetrate and govern. That through this medium they do act, inconspicuously but most powerfully, on the labouring class will probably be admitted. It cannot, I am afraid, with truth be denied, that the principle, "Every man for himself"—or, to say the least, every family and order for itself—of which mistresses complain so loudly when it is adopted by servants, but upon which they too commonly rule their own households, is by their example extended into circles far beyond the range of their direct and conscious influence. The want of hearty sympathy, not only between the classes which are divided by broad and easily recognised distinctions, but between those which are separated by lines so shadowy that, looked at from above or below, they are scarcely discernible—is one of the most serious impediments to social progress, and it is one which a better and more widely diffused culture might do much to remove. Not, indeed, that the education of youth, even taking the word in its deepest sense, is to be regarded as the only, or even the chief, agency for the improvement of society; but it happens to be the point towards which attention is at this moment directed. We are taught to expect great things from a reform in secondary instruction, and this being so, it is surely reasonable to ask that such reforms as may be possible shall be on the widest basis, not omitting any really important section of society.

It will be understood, I hope, that those who make this appeal on behalf of girls, are not proposing the introduction or the enforcement of any particular scheme of instruction. It may be that the curriculum most commonly pursued, or at least professed, is as good as any that is likely to be devised, and that we only want better methods and more encouragement. On questions of detail we are not in the least inclined to dogmatise. It would be rash indeed to fix upon any particular course of instruction as absolutely the best for girls, while as to that of boys, on which so much more thought has been bestowed, we are still in a state of confusion and bewilderment. There seems to be as yet no body of opinion formed out of the floating mass, unanimous enough to be authoritative and competent to pronounce upon what branches of study are in themselves most worthy, what are most useful as educational instruments, what proportion of time should be allotted to each, and the many other complicated questions which must be answered before a perfect scheme of education can be produced. When that happy discovery shall at last have been made, it will probably be found also that the same course is, in the main, the best for both boys and girls, the object being substantially the same, that of awakening and strengthening and adorning the human spirit. That this great work should at least be well *begun* during the period allotted to secondary instruction, is especially necessary in the case of women, because with this first stage their education ends. I do not mean, of course, that a girl necessarily lays aside all study on leaving school, any more than a man does on taking his degree, but that the end of the school course is the same kind of educational terminus to a woman that graduation is to a man. When a girl leaves school, her strictly professional studies assume a greater prominence. In using the word professional, I do not refer to any trade or business, but to the profession which absorbs the great majority of women, that of marriage. For this calling, some technical preparation is required. The amount cannot be great, as under existing social arrangements a thorough acquaintance with needlework and cookery—the very easiest of arts—includes I believe all the special knowledge required by the mistress of a household. But setting aside the question, whether it is desirable that the merely professional training should begin so early—"the second and finishing stage of a liberal education" being altogether omitted—it seems obvious enough, that if regular, methodical instruction is to cease at the age of eighteen, it is the more imperative that the culture, up to that period, should be wide and deep and *humane* in the highest possible degree. A man has some chance of making up at the University the deficiencies of his school training; or if he passes direct from school to business, there is a possibility that he may find in his daily work something of the mental and moral discipline that he needs. But a girl who leaves school unawakened, is not likely to be roused from her lethargy by anything in her home life. The dissipation to which, in the absence of any spur to wholesome activity, so many girls give themselves up, completes the deadening process begun at school.

I have endeavoured to set forth, very imperfectly, but at least without exaggeration, some of the reasons for devoting to this subject more attention than has hitherto been bestowed upon it. Once again I would venture to urge, with the utmost insistance, that it is not a "woman's question." Let me entreat thinking men to dismiss from their minds the belief, that this is a thing with which they have no concern. They cannot help exerting a most serious influence upon it. Silence sometimes teaches more eloquently than words, and while they refrain from giving encouragement, their apparent indifference damps and chills. The matter is in their hands, whether they choose it or not. So long as they thrust it aside, it will not come before the mind of the nation as worthy of serious thought. The Scriptural maxim, "That the soul be without knowledge is not good," will still be interpreted as applying to the souls of men only. We want to have the question settled. If the proposition, often enough vaguely affirmed, that the true greatness of a nation depends as much on its women as on its men, be anything more than a rhetorical flourish, let it be acted upon. Let it be accepted as a fact, if it be a fact, and if not, let it be contradicted and disproved,

Questions relating to Women

that in so far as education is worth anything at all, it is just as desirable for girls as it is for boys. We have little fear but that when once the question gets its fair share of consideration, something, and probably the right thing, will be done. Some efforts have indeed already been made, and so far as they have gone, the results have been encouraging. In London, the Ladies' Colleges, in which men of the highest ability take part, have done much, not only within their own walls but by their influence over other teachers, to raise the standard and improve the tone of education generally. In the country, we have the school at Chantry, near Frome, founded in 1857 by Mr. Allen and Mr. Fussell—the training-school for governesses at Bolham, in Devonshire, where "teaching to teach" is made a prominent study—Miss Clough's school at Ambleside—and others of greater or less importance, all steps in the right direction. But these isolated attempts require to be followed up. The provision of secondary instruction for girls is impeded by the usual hindrance, the want of funds. It is found very difficult to supply really good teaching on such terms as middle-class parents are able and willing to pay, and there is scarcely any assistance forthcoming in the shape of old endowments. The 547 ancient Grammar schools scattered throughout England are, as is well known, almost entirely filled by boys. The other endowed schools, of which there are about 2000, take in a much larger proportion of girls, but they are of the poorer class. The endowed schools which are attended by pupils of the upper and middle classes do not include girls. It may be a question for consideration whether some of these endowments might not, without much divergence from the intentions of the original donors, be used for the foundation of a few first-rate girls' schools, or in some other way be made available for the advancement of female education. At any rate wherever a new institution, such for instance as the Albert Memorial School, in Suffolk, is being founded, it would seem reasonable to make a fair division of the funds, of course taking into consideration any special local circumstances. Again, where we have a St. Nicolas' College, or a first-rate proprietary school, for boys, let there be some corresponding foundation for girls. Let schemes of examination and inspection designed to raise the character of boys' schools be extended to girls also.* In a word let female education be *encouraged*—let it be understood that the public really *cares* whether the work is done well or ill—and the minor practical questions will ere long find for themselves a satisfactory solution.

---

* This has already been done in Scotland. The University of Edinburgh, in instituting a scheme of Local Examinations similar to those of Oxford and Cambridge, offers the same advantages to boys and girls without distinction.

Some account of a proposed new College for women.

[*The following paper was read at the Annual Meeting of the National Association for the Promotion of Social Science*, 1868. *Some passages, inappropriate at the present date, are now omitted.—March*, 1872.]

ON first hearing of a new undertaking, and especially of one involving a large expenditure of time and thought and money, prudent people are put on their guard. They assume an attitude of self-defence. They decline to commit themselves hastily, and before promising their support they require to be assured, first, that there is a real want to be met; secondly, that the new thing proposed is calculated to meet the want; and thirdly, that there is a fair prospect of its being carried into effect.

In the following paper it is proposed to show what the deficiency is which the new College for women is designed to supply, to describe the plan of the institution, and to give some information as to the means by which it is hoped to carry out the scheme.

The alleged want is that of some provision for the education of women above the age of eighteen, analogous to that afforded by the Universities to young men. That any such provision already exists will probably not be affirmed. In order, however, to make this point quite clear from the outset, it may be worth while to quote the evidence of the

Assistant-Commissioner for the London district under the Schools' Inquiry Commission, part of whose business it was to investigate the condition of the secondary education, or in other words, the higher school education of girls. Mr. Fearon says:—

"The *secondary education* of girls is that of girls whose general education is intended to last beyond their 12-13th year of age. But how long is it to last? At what age of the pupil does it merge into the *superior education*? Is there, indeed, in this country any regular system of superior education for girls? And if so, at what age does it begin, what is the course of study which it embraces, and in what institutions is it carried on? . . In the case of boys, such a question is easily answered. The Universities afford them the superior education—the most ancient, the most respected, and, in every sense of the word, the highest educational force in the country. There is, therefore, no difficulty in defining, in the case of boys, where secondary education ends. But in the case of girls the difficulty seems to me insuperable. I have been really quite unable, during the course of my brief inquiry, to discover where in London the superior education of girls is conducted in any such regular and systematic way that it could be recognised by a Commission. . . . If superior education of young women —that is, an education in language, mathematics, and physical science, parallel and equal to that afforded by Oxford and Cambridge to young men—exists at all in London, it exists in private or domestic tuition, and not in any institution which I can discover." *

It is needless to add, that if such an institution is not to be found in London, it certainly will not be found anywhere in England.

It is one thing, however, to show that a thing is absent, and quite another to show that it ought to

* Report of Schools Inquiry Commission, Vol. vii., pp. 381-382.

be present. Those who doubt whether University education is desirable for women, are probably influenced by one or other of the following considerations. Either they hold that though there are no public institutions for women like Oxford and Cambridge, superior instruction is provided by private and domestic tuition, or by some other means, for those who want it; or, that it might be, in some better way than by the foundation of a college; or, that all this talk about education is a mistake. Women have done very well without it hitherto. And when you have made them so learned, what will they be the better for it?

It will be convenient to deal with these widely different views separately.

And first, as to the teaching and the opportunities for study which are available in ordinary homes. It is scarcely necessary to argue at length the question whether superior education is satisfactorily provided for by domestic tuition. The answer will depend on the view taken as to what superior education is, and on the particular cases which have come under any one's notice. In those rare families where the mother has been highly educated, or where the father has both the ability and the leisure to direct the daughter's studies; or where money is abundant, and costly teaching, books, private rooms for study, and cultivated society, can be provided *ad libitum*, young women no doubt have great opportunity of self-improvement. Even in these favoured cases, the absence of a system of discipline, the distractions of society, and the want of the sympathy of numbers must add considerably to the difficulty of steady, fruitful work. But taking such instances at their best, they are too exceptional to form the basis of argument. The best mothers will be the first to admit their own incompetency to carry on the education of their daughters to a high point. Fathers are too busy to take more than a very general sympathetic interest in their daughters' pursuits. That they should undertake the direction of their daily studies is out of the question. And even where there is wealth enough to pay for unlimited lessons, it is only in large towns—one might almost say, only in London and at the Universities—that teachers of the highest rank are to be found.

The most conclusive reply, however, to this view is to be found in the universal admission, that " something is wanted for governesses." Every one agrees that there is no class of schoolmistresses or governesses at all answering to the masters in public schools and private tutors; and that there is no existing provision for the gradual formation of such a class. And if so much as this is conceded, the whole case is conceded. For if there is no adequate provision for the superior instruction of governesses, manifestly there is none for women in general. The conclusion follows—if neither governesses nor mothers *know*, how can they teach? So long as education is not provided *for* them, how can it be provided *by* them?

If, however, it is admitted that with the existing means and appliances, anything at all equivalent to a University education cannot be carried on in ordinary homes, it may still be urged that the main objects in view might be attained by less costly and elaborate means than that of establishing a great central institution, the very idea of which is a novelty, and to some minds an offence. Might not we get all that is essential by higher examinations, by the improvement of girls' schools, and perhaps the extension of the school period, or by supplying courses of lectures in all our large towns?

In considering the first expedient proposed—that of a system of advanced examinations—it is necessary to recall attention to the fact that the deficiency complained of is that of superior *education*, and that examinations, however valuable and necessary in their place, are not education. It is possible to be thoroughly well educated without ever passing an examination, but it is not possible for an uneducated person to pass a good examination. As a stimulus, and as testing and certifying the results of instruction, examinations are most useful, but they are a means, not an end, and must always hold a subordinate place. To suppose that examinations will do instead of teaching, is like supposing that, given the assaying process, you can make a sovereign without extracting the gold from the ore. If we want sovereigns, we must first get the gold, then try it and stamp it. If we want education, we must first teach, then examine and certify. The test and the stamp cannot serve as a substitute for the thing to be tested and stamped.

The suggestion to seek for the higher education of women by improving and developing the existing schools rests on a very different basis. At first sight, it certainly appears to be a very simple and in many respects satisfactory arrangement, to keep girls on longer at school, giving them gradually, as they grow older, a little more freedom and independence, and getting good masters for them in the higher subjects in proportion to their advancement. This would, in fact, be pursuing the present system of finishing schools, only that, as it may be urged, what is now often shallow and pretentious might be made real and thorough. This simple expedient seems to have so much to recommend it, that it is worth while to consider carefully whether it might not be made to answer the purpose in view. For this, it is necessary to know something of the present state of the schools, and of the means suggested for improving them. On these points, the most comprehensive body of information extant is contained in the Report of the Royal Schools Inquiry Commission, and in the evidence laid before them. In their General Report, the Commissioners, after mentioning the various sources from which they obtained evidence, observe that :—

" The general deficiency in girls' education is stated with the utmost confidence, and with entire agreement, with whatever difference of words, by many witnesses of authority. Want of thoroughness and foundation; want of system; slovenliness and showy superficiality; inattention to rudiments; undue time given to accomplishments, and those not taught intelligently or in any scientific manner; want of organization; these may sufficiently indicate the character of the complaints we have received in their most general aspect."*

* Reports, Vol. I., p. 648.

After giving some details as to the general condition of female education and the various measures suggested for its amendment, the Commissioners advert to the proposal for the establishment of a new College, " designed to hold in relation to girls' schools and home teaching a position analogous to that occupied by the Universities towards the public schools for boys," and express their " cordial approval of the object aimed at in this proposal."

The Assistant-Commissioners, "appointed to examine into the education in certain selected districts," give detailed information as to the quality of the teaching in girls' schools, the causes of its defectiveness, and the remedies.

Mr. Stanton, reporting upon the schools of Devon and Somerset, states :—

" That their method of teaching is apt to be desultory and old-fashioned, and they suffer from the want of some guiding principle, which the boys' schools find in the public schools and Universities, to give direction and aim to their studies ; that they suffer more than the boys' schools from the 'finishing' system ; that there is a great want of mistresses and governesses who have been carefully trained for the purpose of tuition."*

Mr. Bompas, the Assistant-Commissioner for Wales, complains that :—

" Mistresses have no means of acquiring that high education which is obtained at the Universities, and which can hardly be obtained, except in a place devoted to the study of the higher branches of knowledge, and strong in the traditions of successive bodies of teachers."†

* Report, Vol. vii., p. 78.   † Ibid.

Proposed new College for women

Mr. Hammond points out that the method of teaching adopted in ladies' schools is propagated by domestic governesses, who have only their school experience to guide them, and that the kind of education given in girls' schools must therefore account in a great measure for the intellectual merits and defects of all English women in the upper and middle classes. He gives the following account of the intellectual results which the best education attainable at a girls' school in his district (Norfolk and Northumberland) might be expected, under favourable circumstances, to produce.

"A cultivated young lady would read and write well, would be faultless in her spelling, and would perform the several arithmetical operations, up to compound division or practice, with tolerable correctness. In addition to the accomplishments —music, drawing, and dancing—she would possess much miscellaneous information, more or less useful; a fair acquaintance with French; a facility of expression and composition in her own language, greater than that possessed by most men of her class of life; and lastly, some knowledge, acquired chiefly at second-hand, of standard English authors. Within certain limits, her general intelligence and her imaginative faculty would be more nimble and active in their play than a man's would be; she would take a more lively view of familiar and domestic incidents, and would extract more pleasure from light and elegant literature. But the study of solid and weighty writers, and the discussion of matters of first-rate importance, would be uninteresting to her, owing to her lack of real comprehensive knowledge, and, consequently, of speculative power. Or, if she attempted to interest herself in such matters, the want of a trained judgment and the imperfect development of her critical and reasoning faculties would oblige her to rely with blind credulity upon the dogmatic assertions of those about her."*

* Report, Vol. viii., pp. 529, 530.

Questions relating to Women

Of the education given in the Yorkshire schools, Mr. Fitch observes :—

"The course of instruction for elder pupils seems to me especially defective; there is nothing bracing or disciplinal in it. No part of it challenges the learner's close attention, or calls upon her for the concentration of all her powers. There are few intellectual difficulties to master. The higher or philosophical aspect of school studies is never presented to her. She is often interested in literature, and reads Shakespeare or Milton with pleasure; but she is never invited to study a poem critically, or examine its archaic words, to hunt out all its allusions, or exhaust its meaning. Even in the best schools, the highest ideal seems to be to produce ' well informed women ; ' but it does not enter into the scheme to make them thinkers, or to encourage the pursuit of truth as truth. And if the reproach be just, that women do not reason accurately, and that their knowledge, even when they possess it, is deficient in organic unity, in coherence and in depth, there is no need to look for any recondite explanation of the fact. The state of the schools in which they are educated sufficiently explains it."*

The Assistant-Commissioner for Lancashire, Mr. Bryce, reports that : —

"Institutions are wanted which should give to women the same opportunity of obtaining the higher education which the Universities give to boys. At present, if a girl learns anything more than what school teaches her . . . she learns it by herself from books, under the disadvantage of having no one to guide her study, no means of testing her progress, no goal or external reward to look forward to ; above all, no oral teaching either to convey knowledge to her, or to excite that intellectual ardour which is so much more precious than any quantity of knowledge . . . . Hence, almost all women have to remain content with what school has taught them, picking up more or less from books according to their acuteness, but without the means of following out any study systematically, since they have not been so much as taught how to study."†

* Report, Vol. ix., pp. 295, 296.   † Ibid., Vol. ix, pp. 337, 838.

Proposed new College for women

The necessity of *beginning at the top*—of teaching not only teachers, but all the women who may eventually become teachers, is urged with much emphasis by Mr. Fearon :—

" Culture," he says, " must begin from above, and work downwards, operating first on those who have to diffuse it, and make knowledge more general and more cheap than it has been among women. We must begin by teaching not only all the actual, but all the possible teachers, that is, women at large . . . Until the higher education is amply provided, and the results of that education are authoritatively tested, there will be no adequate supply of well-informed governesses."*

A mass of evidence to a similar effect is to be found in these most interesting Blue-books.

On this particular point, however, that of the competency of ladies' schools to supply superior education, there is another body of witnesses to whom no less attention is due. These witnesses are the mistresses of the schools. If any one might be expected to stand up for things as they are, and to proclaim the adequacy of existing means, clearly it is the persons who provide those means, namely, schoolmistresses and governesses. One can imagine them saying—one would rather expect them to say —Why go about to start new things? Young women who are anxious to learn can be taught at school. As it is, they are taken away from us just as they are beginning to care for the higher studies. Only let us keep them two or three years longer, and we will provide advanced instruction for them.

* Ibid., Vol. vii., pp. 394, 395.

This will be quite as good for them, and much less troublesome and costly than setting up a new institution.

This is what the teachers of girls might be expected to say. Let us hear what they *do* say. In July, 1867, a memorial was presented to the Educational Commission already referred to, setting forth a deficiency in the education of women, which (it is urged) "it is not in the power of private teachers, however able and zealous, to supply," namely, that of "adequate means and inducements for continuing study beyond the school period." The memorialists admit that there is room for improvement in the earlier stages of education, but they hold that "such improvement might most reasonably be expected from the offer of increased facilities to persons who are about to become teachers for carrying on their studies to a high point, together with some satisfactory means of discriminating between those who are qualified for their work and those who are not." They express their belief that "opportunities of undergoing a course of instruction and discipline adapted to advanced students, combined with examinations testing and attesting the quality of the education received," would be eagerly welcomed, and that the foundation of a place of education for adult female students, at which certificates should be conferred by an independent authority, and to which scholarships and exhibitions should be attached, is among the most urgent educational wants of the present time."

Proposed new College for women

This memorial was signed by 521 teachers of girls, and supported by a large number of ladies and gentlemen specially interested in education.

Another expedient for providing superior instruction must here be touched upon. It is suggested that by establishing in all the large towns systematic courses of lectures, not popular, but genuinely educational, and supplemented by examinations, women might be supplied with instruction of a high class at a cheap rate, without the difficulties involved in leaving home. There is much to be said in favour of this plan, calculated as it is to give valuable aid to a large and important class. But while recognising the usefulness of the lecture system in places where it can be efficiently carried out, and for persons who either cannot afford the expense of residence at College, or who are by other circumstances prevented from leaving home even for the short period of the academical year, one cannot help asking whether any one would be satisfied with lectures *alone* for men. Would any of us wish to see the Colleges at Oxford and Cambridge altogether abolished, and their revenues expended in maintaining Professors who should do nothing but lecture? So extreme a measure would scarcely be recommended by the most thoroughgoing University reformers. But without going further into this question, it will be enough here to point out that whatever may be the advantages of the lecture system, it cannot reach the great mass of young women of the upper class. It is not merely that it cannot do all that is wanted. It cannot do anything at all for the rural districts. Unless the demand for instruction were much more intense and more diffused than it is likely to be in England for many years to come, there would be no chance of keeping up classes for students numerous enough to maintain a staff of qualified lecturers anywhere but in the larger towns. While, therefore, it is much to be desired, that in all the great centres of wealth and industry, institutions similar to the Owens College at Manchester should be established, for the sake of affording to those whose circumstances preclude them from the advantages belonging to residence in a College all the help in self-culture which can be gained by attendance at classes, we must not suppose that any such machinery will meet the wants of the sisters of the young men who go to Oxford and Cambridge. The Universities are not fed, in any considerable proportion, by the great manufacturing towns. The two thousand sisters of the two thousand undergraduates who, at any given time, are under instruction at Cambridge, will be found for the most part scattered about in country houses and parsonages, and in the families of professional men and retired merchants and manufacturers in the villages and smaller towns all over England and Wales and Scotland. They live in the country, out of sight, and it is not their way to make a great noise. And so, naturally enough, the dwellers in the important bustling towns are apt to forget their existence. But, if we would consider, these obscure and silent people are exactly the class of women whom it is worth while to remember. Their abundant leisure and many opportunities of influence have hitherto been turned to small account. Yet how much might be made of them! The Hall and the Rectory are the centres of light for a whole parish. If their light be darkness, how great is that darkness!

But here we arrive at the fundamental question, whether, after all, light is better than darkness— whether a moderately ignorant person cannot discharge the plain duties of life just as well as the most highly educated—whether, in trying to work women up to an exalted pitch of mental superiority, we might not be making sacrifices of health, refinement of manners, and the minor morals, for which no intellectual gains could compensate.

This fundamental question is as broad as it is deep, and requires to be surveyed in many different aspects, if we would arrive at a true solution.

And first, let us be clear as to what the alternative is. Let it be distinctly understood that the choice is not between a life wholly given up to study, and a life spent in active domestic duty. The dilemma thus stated is untrue on both sides; for while on the one hand, giving to women the opportunity of a complete education does not mean that they will thereupon spend all their lives in reading, so, on the other, denying them education does not mean that they will occupy themselves in household affairs. The young unmarried women of the present generation are not called upon to take an active part in household work. It is needless to insist on this, for every one knows it, and yet there is an undertone of lamentation and reproach as the admission is made. There is nothing for them to do, we confess; and yet somehow we have a feeling that they ought to be doing it. We sigh, and say—Yes, domestic employments are gone out of fashion. But why have they gone out of fashion? There are two reasons—the increase of wealth, and the supply of domestic wants by machinery. There are more families of a condition to keep a staff of servants, and a great deal of what used to be done by hand at home is now done, in whole or in part, by machinery in workshops and factories. "Ready-made" has taken the place of "home-made." There is less work to do, and there are more servants to do it. It may be, that in this instance the principle of the division of labour which rules modern life has been pushed too far. It might be better if ladies took some share in household work, superintended the servants more, and gave *them* also some time which they could call their own for reading and recreation. And in large families, where means are not abundant, sensible women still find things to do which " save the servants," and so save money. But in the upper middle class the need for this is exceptional, and in any case, the time so spent is but a small portion taken out of the day. The fact is patent, that unless we came to dismissing the servants —by which we should sacrifice one of the most precious civilising influences which modern society affords— a healthy young woman will find no adequate pull upon her energies in the domestic employments of a well-to-do household. If any imaginative persons should still insist that there may, might, *must*, be plenty of household work for ladies if they would only do it, it will at any rate be admitted that they are *not* doing it. None of us— or only a very few people, the quality of whose optimism is somewhat strained—profess to be satisfied with the present manner of life of young women of the wealthy class. The young lady of the world is universally condemned. No one will give her a good word. She gets neither praise nor pity, still less sympathy or help. We are all agreed that the sooner she is abolished the better.

But what are we to have in her place? That is the question. We are quite ready, it may be said, to crush the gay trifler, but we are not prepared to accept in her stead the pale-faced student, poring over miserable books. We want healthy, happy, dutiful English women; and we are persuaded that if women take to College, and examinations, and diplomas, and the rest, they will be unhealthy, unhappy, undutiful, and worst of all—American.

But what if it should be found that it is through the process of poring over books—in due season, with moderation, and under wise guidance—that health, and happiness, and dutifulness, and the many good things which go to make an English lady of the highest type, will most surely come?

What is so conducive to health and happiness as regular, interesting occupation? Who are so likely

to see the true poetry which lies in the discharge of
the humblest duties as those whose minds are fitly
balanced, their imaginations withdrawn from vanities,
and occupied with pure visions? What is so likely
to give gentleness, simplicity, and real refinement, as
an orderly, melodious, disciplined life, possessing a
genuine dignity which does not need to support
itself by defiance? Self-assertion and false independence are common enough in English society. What
is wanting is the true independence which can oppose
a calm and firm resistance to degrading fashions.
English manners cannot now be held up as a model
to the world. In the towns the restless movement
of modern life threatens to sweep away the stately
grace of quieter times. In the country there is no
hurry; but the habit of pursuing a dull, lethargic
round, only broken by the physical excitements of
out-door life, is not favourable to the growth of self-
respect and mutual deference. In neither case is
there the hearty sincerity, the glow of sympathy,
which ought to mark the social intercourse of people
who call themselves Christians and profess to love
one another. A society in which the

"reverence
Dearer to true young hearts than their own praise,"

will find fit objects on which to bestow itself, in
which the unselfish consideration due to equals will
find occasions for exercise among congenial friends;
where self-consciousness will be absorbed in common
interests, and the common pursuit of aims worthy of
human beings will give a meaning to each detail of

daily life, must surely be a better school of manners
and morals than a narrow monotonous routine of
exertion, without motive and pleasure, which is not
relaxation, a life—

> " That has no ear save for the tickling lute
> Set to small measures—deaf to all the beats
> Of that large music rolling o'er the world."

If, indeed, higher education is regarded merely as
the acquirement of an unusual quantity of information—information which may happen to prove useful,
or may not—there is much reason for scepticism as
to its practical value. So long as education is treated
only as a means of getting on in the world, nothing
is easier than to show that women for whom the
getting on has been done by other people do not
want it. But it is not as a means of getting on that
University education is recommended. The object
of the new College is not to enable women to make
money, though that may probably be among the
results indirectly attained. It has a wider scope.
It has been said of education that its business, "in
respect of knowledge, is not to perfect a learner in
all or any one of the sciences, but to give his mind
that freedom, that disposition, and those habits, that
may enable him to obtain any part of knowledge he
shall apply himself to, or stand in need of, in the
future course of his life." This will be the aim of the
College work. It will not be specifically directed
towards changing the occupations of women, but
rather towards securing that whatever they do shall
be done well. Whether as mistresses of households,
mothers, teachers, or as labourers in art, science,

literature, and notably in the field of philanthropy, so largely occupied by women, their work suffers from the want of previous training. They have to do for themselves in mature life, and in a difficult and abnormal manner, what ought to have been done for them in their youth. They are required to inflict upon themselves the discipline, and to gain for themselves the knowledge, which ought to have come to them as part of their education. Their youth is unduly cut short. They are expected to be grown up at eighteen. And according to the general rule by which human beings do what is expected of them, they *do* grow up, at any rate in the sense that they cease to grow any more. Many a woman is as childish and undeveloped at twenty-eight as she was at eighteen. She has missed the intermediate stage of discipline between the necessary restraint of childhood and early youth, and the undivided responsibility which is the burden of mature years. Is it said that the education of life is more than that of books? That is most true. And if there is any stage in our history at which it is of primary importance that the education of life—in other words, the conditions and circumstances in which we are placed —should be wisely adjusted so as to favour healthy growth, it is surely during the transition period of youth. It is not natural to be "finished" at eighteen. It is when the school period has passed that the mind and character are ready to receive the kind of teaching and discipline which are wanted as a preparation for standing alone. And as has been already

said, there are very few homes which can by any
possibility supply the kind of training which is needed.

When this is understood—when it has been
thoroughly apprehended that University education
is not proposed as a substitute for the education of
life, but as a temporary stage, a preparation for the
duties of life, whatever they may prove to be—it
may be hoped that the fear entertained by some
persons lest secular learning should take the place
of the higher influences of religion will disappear.
There are many who would consider it a less than
doubtful good to have women withdrawn from
philanthropic work, shut up with their books, instead
of helping the sick and poor. But such persons
must remember that thoughtless activity is not the
most fruitful. Zeal is good, but let it be zeal according
to knowledge. We are sometimes reminded that
the Gospel was preached by unlettered fishermen;
but it was not upon the unlettered fishermen that
the condemnation was pronounced—"Woe unto you,
for ye have taken away the key of knowledge; ye
entered not in yourselves, and them that were entering
in ye hindered."

And who among those early preachers laboured
more zealously, more successfully, in season and out
of season, than that Apostle of whom it was said that
much learning had made him mad? His culture
had not made him cold and selfish—a heartless
Epicurean. Rather it was by the diligent study of
the things which aforetime were written for our
learning, that in him the springs of hope were fed.

We have no right to suppose that we of later times can do without learning—that we can be "thoroughly furnished unto all good works" if we take no pains about the furnishing. The duties of life are not "plain." That stage in a nation's history during which it is passing from barbarism to civilisation is full of perplexities and anomalies. We cannot get rid of them by shutting our eyes. To untie the knots, to solve the difficult problems which the circumstances of our time force upon us, we want all the light which can be gained by the widest diffusion of sound and godly learning. We cannot spare a single ray.

A few words may here find place with respect to the effect of mental cultivation on health. That a heartless, mechanical routine must be morally and spiritually deadening is not difficult to see, but it seems to be commonly supposed that to the physical constitution it is rather strengthening than otherwise. It is, in fact, often taken for granted, that though for women who have only themselves to think of, it may be a good thing to have some intellectual resources, for *mothers* there is nothing like good sound ignorance. A stolid indifference to the higher interests of life, complete absorption in petty cares, is supposed to produce a placid, equable animal state of existence, favourable to the transmission of a healthy constitution to the next generation. We have persuaded ourselves that Englishmen of the present day are such a nervously excitable race, that the only chance for their descendants is to keep the mothers in a state of coma. The fathers, we think, are incurable. Their feverish energy cannot be controlled. We give them up. But there is hope for the future if only mothers can be kept out of the vortex.

But are we, indeed, so morbidly spiritual and intellectual as this notion assumes? Is it because their minds are overwrought, because they have thrown themselves with too great ardour into literary and scientific pursuits, that men and women display so much eagerness in making and spending money? Is it not rather that men heap up and women squander, as a diversion from an insupportable dulness, incapable of higher pleasures?

The theory that starving the brain is the way to keep it healthy, is not supported by medical testimony. A writer on the " Physiology and Pathology of the Mind "—Dr. Maudsley—treating of the effect of education as predisposing, or the reverse, to insanity, urges the need of such training for women as would strengthen and develope the character. Of the present system of female education, Dr. Maudsley observes that it is hardly necessary to point out how ill adapted it is—

" to store the mind with useful knowledge, and to train up a strong character. It is peculiarly fitted for the frivolous purposes of female life; but that it is so is its greatest condemnation. As the education of women is widened, deepened, and improved, other and better resources will be discovered and earnestly used, and the reaction of a higher mode of life on female education and female nature cannot fail to be most beneficial."*

*   *   *   *   *

* See " The Physiology and Pathology of the Mind," Part II., chap. i., On the Causes of Insanity; par. Education.

A word may here be said with regard to endowments. In the Report of the Royal Commission already quoted, Colleges are spoken of as fit objects for encouragement, either by the Crown or by Parliament. It is not very likely, however, that either the Crown or Parliament, or any public body will give effective encouragement to the undertaking so long as it can be called an experiment. It cannot be denied that an institution for women, professing to give something equivalent to an Oxford or Cambridge education, is a new thing, and public bodies will think it only right to wait till it has succeeded, before doing much to help it on. At the same time, the persons most competent to judge insist that female education is not yet in a position to do without external aid. For male education large funds are already provided, and are being continually increased. For the education of women (except those of the labouring class) scarcely any public provision is made, and in some notable cases the tendency has been to divert to other uses what was intended for this purpose. Education supplies many illustrations of the saying, "To him that hath, more shall be given, and from him that hath not, shall be taken away even that he hath." There are indications, however, that the tide is turning, and it is at this juncture specially important that the friends of education should take the preliminary steps necessary to secure that, in any redistribution of endowments, a fair share should be applied to providing for the superior education of women. The initiative must be taken by private persons, and something like a start must be made before any definite application can be preferred for grants from public funds. When the first step shall have been taken, and a nucleus formed, there is little doubt that benefactions in various shapes will accrue. In this point of view, every contribution to such an undertaking as the new College will have a kind of reproductive power. Those who take part in promoting the scheme at its present stage, not only help to bring a useful institution into existence,—they are putting their hands to a work which will by-and-by be carried on to far larger issues. It was begun in faith and hope in more difficult times than ours. Those who went before have prepared the way; we profit by their labours. It is for us to do our part, while handing on the task to the generations yet to come.

On the Influence upon Girls' Schools of External Examinations.

[*The London Student, May*, 1868.]

EVERYBODY is aware how rapidly of late years schemes of examination have been multiplied and extended. Some timid souls regard them as an incubus upon the land, a charge, and a mischievous charge, upon the freedom and the energies of young life. "You will examine people out of all their knowledge," says one. "Life will soon be altogether spent in examining, being examined, or showing cause why you have not been examined," says another. The superstitious, on the other side, attach an unreasoning and unreasonable value to examinations. They are to be the grand cure of all educational ailments, to give tone and vigour to intellectual feebleness, to develop and train to their utmost perfection all latent faculties and energies. In the eyes of some, the present passion for examinations is a mere fashionable craze, which will have its day; in the minds of others, it is the inauguration of the reign of right reason and sound judgment in matters of education. Without rushing to either extreme, it may be safe to commit ourselves to the very general proposition, that for good or for evil, probably for both, methods and plans of examination do constitute one of the most powerful forces in our modern systems of education.

It may not be out of place to remark, however, that the use of examinations is no wonderful discovery of the nineteenth century. So long as there have been real teachers in the world, so long have they sought by the best methods they could devise to test and try their pupils, to discover the mental condition of each, how far they were passive recipients of another's ideas, or, less even than that, how far they were fellow-workers with their teachers. Now, whatever method the teacher may have chosen —and such methods are susceptible of almost infinite variation—the thing endeavoured has been one and the same—examination. There is one grand advantage of the lecture over the book, of the living teacher over the dead printed matter—that examination can proceed *pari passu* with direct instruction, which, if possible it exceeds in value and importance. When a book can ask and answer questions, when it can respond to the clouded, doubtful, puzzled look, or to the anxious inflections of the voice, then may we dispense with the living teacher, and then and not till then may we dismiss as unprofitable all inquiries into the just value (as also into the wisest methods) of examination. Seen from this point of view, the teacher is the examiner, *the examiner, the teacher*, a double function consentaneous and coincident.

It is not, however, as a *direct* instrument of teaching that we propose now to consider the influence of examinations. Those which alone come before the eye of the public have altogether another scope and purpose. Not that they do not (or may not) teach much directly, and indirectly even more; but that their special end is to test achieved results, not to help in the achieving, and to weigh in the balance alike the teacher and the taught. That this is necessary who can doubt? So long as teachers are but mortals they will blunder, and, sorrowful to say, will repeat their blunders, which of their own unaided vision they are not likely to detect, the mental twist or crotchet which caused the original deflection disqualifying for its discovery.

So far then from the teacher being the best judge of the results of his teaching, he is usually the very worst; and it would not be too much to lay it down as a first principle in all examinations of results, that no teacher can rightly be a judge of his own teaching, no *body* of teachers of their own teaching. This principle, which applies equally to the highest and to the lowest, necessitates the provision of external tests, such as, to take the instances best known to all of us, and of easiest application to the case of girls, those provided by the University of Cambridge in the Local Examinations.

But why, it may be asked, seek to test achieved results at all? Life will sufficiently prove and try them for us. Perhaps if we considered the case of individual students only, it might be possible to assent to this, though even then it would be fair to urge that the test of life comes too late to be of practical value.

The superficial knowledge and real ignorance which a well-considered examination would have exposed at a period when they might yet have been remedied, find too terrible a Nemesis when left to be corrected by the course of life and the progress of events. It is hard to find oneself less accurate, less ready, less able than one took oneself to be. It is better to know this, to take the just measure of one's attainments, than to be surprised hereafter by a sudden perception of mortifying and irremediable incapacity. The keen sense of power which seems specially to belong to the period of the rapidly-developing faculties, needs to be thus chastened by the test of practical work within clearly defined limits. Untried and inexperienced, we feel capable of all things; failure teaches us modesty and charity.

The advantages, however, of systematic and practical examination are by no means confined to those who are directly submitted to it. In the case of schools sending in candidates to the Local Examinations, the candidates, their fellow-pupils, and their teachers are all more or less benefited; and this would be still more largely the case if the examination, instead of being the conclusion of the school career, could be made an ordinary and regular incident during its continuance. This view is little likely to find favour with University men already over-weighted with examining work, but it can scarcely fail to commend itself to teachers. External examinations have been spoken of as designed to test achieved results; but these results are not supposed to be final.

One grand advantage is the increased steadiness of school-work. Every teacher knows how difficult it is in the present confused state of the education of girls, to work out intelligently a comprehensive plan, which shall combine breadth of general principle with thoroughness and accuracy of detail. Our material is imperfect, our machinery faulty, our motive power fitful and irregular. We have neither perfect pupils, perfect methods, nor, reluctant as we may be to confess it, perfect teachers. We are constantly liable to fail and falter through difficulties arising out of the foolishness of parents, the perversity of pupils, and our own ignorance and indolence.

So long as this is the case, we may well be thankful to accept such support as any well-devised scheme of examination gives us. In the steady endeavour after a clearly defined standard, we are more likely to attain the best educational results, than in working according to ever-varying standards, or to no standard at all. And to say this is by no means to fall into the mistake of making examination regulations the measure, and literal conformity with them the end, of all our teaching. A right apprehension of the spirit does away with all bondage to the letter. Within the prescribed limits there is abundant room for the highest originality of method, and the utmost fertility of invention of any teacher; and if the limits be too narrow, by all means let them be extended—. only let what is done be well done. This steadying influence is an advantage to pupils no less than to teachers. Whilst the place in the class list is of the least possible moment, the habit of accurate and thoughtful work, and the perception of the difference between knowing a thing and knowing about it, are of incalculable importance, and we are fully sustained in our belief that great support and stimulus are afforded to the young student by the knowledge that her work will be submitted to an independent and impartial tribunal. This advantage is not confined to candidates actually sent in for examination, but is a gain more or less to the whole school. Those unwise teachers who prepare individual pupils for examination by that mysterious process called "cramming," forfeit, and deservedly so, this advantage. But it is surely unnecessary to do more by way of exposing this folly than to point out the hopeless confusion of such teachers as to what are the ends and what only the means of education.

Cramming is, moreover, as absolutely unnecessary for the purposes of examination as it is mischievous morally and intellectually. Many of the most successful candidates from girls' schools have, to our certain knowledge, gone in without one hour of special preparation from the ordinary work of their class. Where this is the case, the influence upon the school is likely to be the best and strongest. A generous emulation is awakened, which has its root in sympathy, not in envious rivalry; and the success of one issues in the increased energy and application of her companions; the defeat of another in their greater thoroughness and accuracy. The precision in working secured thus to the school is invaluable.

It may be worth while here to remark that the predictions of those who expected that the opening of these examinations to girls would introduce jealousies, heart-burnings, and dissensions unknown before, have so far been curiously falsified by the results. Whether we are to attribute it to the *moral* effects of the mental discipline involved in the attempt at real study, or to whatever other cause, the fact is certain, that the simplicity, sweetness, and good feeling of the girl candidates have hitherto been as remarkable as their orderliness and diligence. It has been pleasant to see the way in which they "fraternise" with each other, and how eager they are in all acts and offices of kindness. And here lies a great though altogether incidental advantage of such examinations. They tend to draw schools and teachers together and to break down the painful isolation hitherto so characteristic of the profession of schoolmistresses. The internal economy, the organization of no school is interfered with, yet each begins to regard itself, and to be regarded, no longer as a solitary organisation, but as a member of the great community of schools: each teacher as a member of the community of teachers. Now this, in the present state of things, is clear gain; there is no need that we should become pedantic and professional. There is every need that we should exchange thought, experience, sympathy. Many of our greatest difficulties as teachers will be removed when once we have learnt to trust each other fully, and to work together heartily. Then indeed we may hope to secure that just economy of teaching power, that wise distribution of forces, without which it is vain to look forward to any great advance in the education of girls. It is quite possible that such a result might have been brought about in one or other of many different ways. In any case there would have been needed some such bond of unity amidst infinite diversity as is afforded by the very nature of this common test. The interest taken by parents in the examinations has also been so great as to encourage the hope that English fathers and mothers do not intend, when they delegate their functions as educators to the professional teacher, to dismiss all serious care for the education of their daughters. We need not merely a closer union amongst teachers, but a greater sympathy and a fuller co-operation between parents and teachers.

But it will be said in all this, you have assumed the perfection of present schemes of examination, whereas we all know . . . . . Yes, we all know the inherent and inevitable imperfection of all things human. No perfect scheme of examination has yet been devised, or being devised, could be carried into effect. A test which, being uniform for all, must press unequally upon individuals of diverse capacities and powers, which gauges only some of the intellectual results, and is incapable of direct application to the moral results of education, how incomplete and defective this must be! We can only say that, so far as it goes, it is of inestimable value, and that it is one of the most foolish of all foolish objections to a thing good in itself, that it does not do something which it was never intended to do.

The ideally perfect examination has yet to be devised. Meanwhile, the University Local Examinations combine many of the most important requisites of such an examination. A standard of average attainments, pitched not at all too high for average ability and average industry; free play for special aptitudes and special attainments; methods devised to test, and on the whole pretty fairly, not only the memory, but the imagination and the judgment; absolute fairness and impartiality,—these are secured to us by the very structure of the examinations. What of disadvantage attaches itself to them would seem to be chiefly the fault of teachers themselves. If these will confound means with ends, ignore the value of time in education, and try by cramming to crowd the work of years into months; stereotype their teaching to the dead level of a pass, or unduly press the eager and ambitious with a view to honours, on them be the shame, as theirs alone is the folly. To those who know how rightly to use them, such examinations are of the highest advantage; only let it be borne in mind, that these are not to be suffered to become the one determining force in education—

that as the machinery becomes more highly wrought and finished, it will be ever more and more our duty to see that it is set in motion of the informing spirit.

Special Systems of Education for Women.

[*The London Student, June,* 1868.]

AMONG the controversies to which the movement for
improving the education of women has given rise,
there is one which presses for settlement. The
question has arisen and must be answered—Is the
improved education which, it is hoped, is about to be
brought within reach of women, to be identical with
that of men, or is it to be as good as possible, but in
some way or other specifically feminine? The form
in which the question practically first presents itself
is—What shall be the standards of examination?
For though there are still a not inconsiderable
number of places of so-called education, into which
no examiners from without are allowed to penetrate,
the persons by whom these establishments are kept
up are pretty certain to disapprove of any change in
the existing practice, and are not likely to be troubled
with perplexing questions as to the direction in which
the reforming tendency should work. The controversy may therefore be assumed to be between two
parties, each equally accepting examinations as
" valuable and indispensable things" alike for women
and for men—each equally admitting that "their
use is limited," and that they may be abused.

Of these two parties, one regards it as essential
that the standards of examination for both sexes
should be the same; the other holds that they may
without harm—perhaps with advantage—be different.

The controversy does not lie between those on the one hand who, believing men and women to be exactly alike, logically hold that all the conditions to which they may be subjected ought to be precisely similar, and those on the other who, regarding them as completely unlike, cannot believe that anything which is good for one sex can be anything but bad for the other. No rational person takes either of these clearly-defined views; but between the two there is a kind of cloudland, in whose dimness it is not always easy to see the way to wise action. It may do something towards clearing away the haze to endeavour to give some answer to the question— Why do you ask for a common standard? Do you want to prove the intellectual equality of the sexes? or their identity? If you desire to improve female education, why not strive after what is ideally best, instead of trying to get things for women which have produced results far short of perfection in men?

The abstract questions as to equality and identity may be quickly dismissed. The advocates of the " common " principle—those who hold what may be called the *humane* theory—altogether disclaim any ambition to assert either. As to what may be expected as the statistical result of comparison by a common standard, there may be much difference of opinion. If it should be to show a general average of somewhat inferior mental strength in women, a fact will have been discovered of some scientific interest perhaps, but surely of no very great importance. That complete similarity should be proved seems in the nature of things impossible, even if there could be any reason for attempting it; for supposing it to be a fact, it is not the sort of fact which could be brought to light by the test of an examination. A comparison between male and female novelists, or male and female poets—if one may venture to apply such epithets to "the double-natured"—would be a better criterion, for those who are curious in such matters, than any which could be devised by examiners. In a discussion of practical policy, these considerations may be set aside as matters of chiefly speculative interest.

We come down, therefore, to the narrower and more hopeful inquiry—Which is best, to extend methods of education admitted to be imperfect, or to invent new ones presumably better?

The latter course is urged on the ground that there are differences between men and women which educational systems ought to recognise; or supposing this to be disputed, that at any rate the conditions of women's lives are special, and ought to be specially prepared for; or there is a latent feeling of repugnance to what may appear like an ungraceful, perhaps childish, attempt to grasp at masculine privileges—an idea which jars upon a refined taste. Considerations of this sort, resting mainly upon sentiment or prejudice, can scarcely be met by argument. It is usually admitted that we are as yet in the dark as to the specific differences between men and women—that we do not know how far they are native, and to what extent those which strike the eye may have been produced by artificial influences—that even if we knew much more than we do about the nature of the material to be dealt with, we should still have much to learn as to the kind of intellectual discipline which might be most suitable. Nor have we as yet any trustworthy evidence—scarcely so much as a plausible suggestion—as to the manner in which the differences of the work in life to which men and women respectively are said to be called, could be met by corresponding differences in mental training. The arbitrary differences established by fashion seem to have been directed by the rule of contraries rather than by any intelligent judgment. Practically, what we come to is something like this—People who want to impose a special system have some theories as to the comparative merits of certain studies, which they feel a friendly impulse to press upon others at every convenient opportunity; or they have a vague impression that as certain subjects and methods have been in a manner set apart for women ever since they can remember, there is most likely something in them which distinguishes them either as suitable to the female mind, or as specially useful to women in practical life. To discover how much of truth there may be behind this opinion would be a tedious and difficult task. It may be enough to remark that experience seems to be against it. It is precisely because the special system, as hitherto tried, has proved a signal failure, that reform is called for.

There are other advocates, however, of independent schemes, who take up a totally different ground.

They only half believe, or perhaps altogether repudiate, the female mind theory; and they are prepared to go great lengths in assimilating the education of the sexes. But they say—1. Male education is in a very bad state—therefore it is not worth while to spread it. 2. Rightly or wrongly, it *is* different from that of women. It would be useless to examine people in things they have not learnt; and women do not as a rule learn Latin and Greek and Mathematics. We must recognise facts.

By all means let us recognise facts. But let us remember also that facts are created things, and mortal. There are old facts, of a bad sort, which want to be put an end to, and there are new and better facts, which may by wise measures be called into being. And speaking of facts, let this be considered—that however bad the education of men may be, that of women is undoubtedly worse. On this point the Report of the Schools Inquiry Commission speaks very distinctly. After adverting to the general deficiency in girls' education, which " is stated with the utmost confidence and with entire agreement, with whatever difference of words, by many witnesses of authority," the Commissioners observe that " the same complaints apply to a great extent to boys' education. But on the whole, the evidence is clear that, not as they might be but as they are, the girls' schools are inferior in this view to the boys' schools." And if this is the evidence as regards the school period, during which girls are receiving more or less regular and systematic instruction, it is likely to be still more unanimous and emphatic as to the later stage, during which men are, in however antiquated and foolish a manner, as the reformers tell us, at any rate in some sort taken in hand by the universities, while women are for the most part left altogether to their own resources. It will probably be admitted, without further argument, that to make the education of average women only as good as that of men, would be a step in advance of what it is now.

But is this intermediate step an indispensable one? Are we obliged to go through a course of wandering along paths which have been found to lead away from the desired end? Cannot we use the light of experience, and, avoiding exploded errors, march straight on to perfection by the nearest road? To a great extent, Yes. There is no reason, for example, to imitate boys' schools in their excessive devotion to physical sports; or in the exclusion of music from the ordinary school routine; or to take up methods of teaching of which the defects have been discovered. Again, looking to the higher stage, no one would wish to reproduce among women either the luxurious idleness of the lower average of university men, or the excessive strain of the competition for honours which is said to act so injuriously on the studious class. But these are evils from which women are pretty securely guarded by existing social conditions. There is at present not much fear that girls will take too much out-of-door exercise, that they will give too little time to music, or that governesses will blindly

model their teaching on the plans in vogue in boys'
schools. Fashionable young ladies are not in danger
of idling away their time at college, and the studious
are not tempted by valuable rewards attached to
academical distinction. It is not in its weak points
that male education is likely to be imitated by
women.

The immediate controversy turns, as has been said,
upon examinations—examinations regarded as a controlling force, directing the course of instruction into
certain channels; pronouncing upon the comparative
value of subjects, fixing the amount of time and
attention bestowed upon each, and to some extent
guiding the method of teaching; wholesomely stimulating; and aptly fulfilling its great function of
plucking. What are the conditions required to produce the right kind of controlling force? We want
authority—that no one disputes. We want the best
subjects encouraged. What they are, the most competent judges have not yet settled; but most people,
perhaps not all, will agree that when they have made
up their minds their verdict ought to be acted upon.
We want an examination which can be worked
beneficially. To adopt an examination so radically
bad that it could not in itself be made an improving
exercise, might be defensible, perhaps even justifiable, taking a very enlarged view of contingent
moral influences. But it would be a difficult case to
defend, and no one has taken it in hand. We want
an examination for which candidates will be forthcoming. Finally, we want an examination which

will sift. We do not want to have certificates of proficiency given to half-educated women. There are examinations which will do this already within reach.

Authority; wise choice of subjects; so much skill in the construction of questions that at any rate they do not invite shallow and unthorough preparation; practicability; and due severity—these are requisites which most people will agree in regarding as essential. But the agreement does not go much farther. As to authority, what constitutes it? Is it the personal reputation of the examiners, or is it their official position? Or is it the prestige acquired by prescription? Or has the quality of the candidates anything to do with it? It is as to the two last points that opinions differ. We can agree so far as this, that an examination by men of high repute will carry more weight than one by men unknown, and that an examination by an official body such as a university, will be more readily believed in than one by any self-constituted board, however respectable. But supposing these two points secured, is a new examination conducted by competent examiners appointed by a university all that is to be desired? Will an unknown standard, having expressly in view candidates drawn from a limited and notoriously illiterate class, be worth much as regards authority? Mr. Matthew Arnold remarks that "High pitched examinations are the result, not the cause, of a high condition of general culture, and examinations tend, in fact, to adjust

themselves to studies." There is much reason to
expect that such a scheme as has been supposed
would from the outset be, whether justly or unjustly,
regarded as in some way accommodated to the inferior attainments of the class, and that starting
with small repute, it would have to contend with
the natural tendency of all things to justify their
character. The most highly cultivated women would
not care to submit themselves to an ordeal in which
to fail might be disgrace, but to pass would be no
distinction. The mere fact of its special character
would in itself repel them. That the greatest of
female novelists should have taken the precaution
to assume a masculine *nom de plume* for the express
purpose of securing their work against being measured by a class standard, is significant of the feeling
entertained by women. Right or wrong, wise or
foolish, here is at any rate a fact to be recognised,
and a fact having a manifest bearing on the question in hand. An examination limited to a class,
and with which the *élite* of that class will have
nothing to do, is not likely to command very high
respect.

As regards the choice of subjects and the practical
manipulation, so to speak, it appears that if we are
to have an examination stamped by official authority,
we must go to the old authorities for it, and these
authorities may be supposed to have already done
their best, according to their light, in devising the
existing examinations. University examiners are
human, and no doubt make mistakes, but if they

are incompetent to direct the education with which they are familiar, why should they become suddenly wise when they enter upon a field unknown to them by experience, but as regards which they are but too well supplied with theories? It may be said that the new work would probably fall into the hands of new men, who would start with more advanced ideas, and that they might be able to carry through for women what they cannot get for men. But the counsels of inexperience are not always the wisest, and supposing the case to be as represented, it seems to be merely a question of a very short time. At the Universities the generations succeed each other much more rapidly than anywhere else. The young men of to-day will be the governing body a few years hence, and will then be able to carry out their ideas for both men and women. If the new thing proposed is better than what men have already, women do not wish to monopolise it.

The questions of practicability and severity may be taken together. A medium is required between a test so far out of reach that no one will go in for it, and one so loose that it fails to discriminate. And here we must not forget that, though without any fault of their own, the great majority of women *are* very imperfectly educated, and it is therefore impossible, in the nature of things, to devise any test which can at once embrace the great mass and yet be sufficiently exclusive. There are a few educated women. We want to find them. We may be very sorry that other women, perhaps equally intelligent and willing, have not had the chance of being educated too. We are bound to do all we can to bring education within their reach. But we are not bound to perpetuate the evils with which we are struggling, by certifying competent knowledge where it does not exist.

And it is not, except perhaps to some small extent, that the education of women has taken a different line, and that they do know some things thoroughly well, if only they had the opportunity of showing it. The defectiveness of female education tells all the way through. The schools are indeed improving, but then it is to be observed that the best girls' schools are precisely those in which the "masculine" subjects have been introduced, and by which therefore the imposition of a feminine test is least likely to be desired. The real question of practicability therefore seems to be, not what would exactly fit female education as it is, but what it may be made to fit itself to, within a reasonable time and without great inconvenience and difficulty.

On this question much valuable evidence is to be found in the Reports of the Schools Inquiry Assistant Commissioners. Mr. Giffard says, "If I were to sum up the impressions I derived from my visits to girls' schools, I should say (1) that the mental training of the best girls' schools is unmistakeably inferior to that of the best boys' schools; (2) that there is no natural inaptitude in girls to deal with any of the subjects which form the staple of a boy's education; (3) that there is no disinclination on the part of the majority of teachers to assimilate the studies of girls to those of boys; (4) that the present inferiority of girls' training is due to the despotism of fashion, or, in other words, the despotism of parents and guardians." Other evidence to the same effect abounds. Any one who knows well the better class of teachers of girls will endorse Mr. Giffard's statement as to their willingness to adopt innovations. There is no insuperable difficulty in getting teaching of any subject where there is sufficient demand for it. It would probably be easier to get first-rate teaching in classics and mathematics than in, say modern languages, because they are the subjects which have hitherto been chiefly cultivated by highly educated men. And though a test which would at first exclude the great majority of ordinary women may have an appearance of rigour almost amounting to cruelty, it is consoling to know that there are already open to women many opportunities of bringing to the test such elementary or fragmentary knowledge as circumstances may have enabled them to pick up. The Society of Arts gives examinations not to be despised, in a great variety of subjects, and the machinery for conducting them brings them within easy reach. The Government Department of Science and Art gives certificates of competency to teach in various branches of science and art. The Royal Academy of Music gives examinations and a diploma. The Home and Colonial School Society holds examinations for governesses, which include, besides the ordinary subjects of instruction, such as modern languages, music and drawing, the special qualifications required by governesses in schools, namely, teaching power, and governing power. It cannot be truly said that female teachers have no means of showing competency, and that those who are willing rather to work gradually for radical reform than to catch hastily at half measures, are sacrificing the present generation for the sake of shadowy advantages in a distant future.

The kind of result which is likely to follow from an adaptation of a female examination to the *examinees*, may be conjectured from the advice given by a schoolmistress in reference to the Cambridge Local Examinations. Complaining of the vexatious demands for a degree of attainment in arithmetic not commonly reached in girls' schools, she remarked briefly, "I would have all that expunged." The suggestion that one advantage of these examinations might consist in the pressure brought to bear in favour of unpopular subjects, was met by the rejoinder, "But why press an unpopular subject which is of no use in after-life?"

The tendency of examinations to adjust themselves to studies is a consideration of great importance. At present the weak points in the education of men are the comparatively strong points in that of women, and therefore less need attention. It is where men are strong that women want stimulus and encouragement—and it may be added, they need this only in order to produce satisfactory results. The Cambridge Local Examinations furnish a case in point. In the first examination to which girls were admitted, 90 per cent. of the senior candidates failed in the preliminary arithmetic. Fortunately, the standard was fixed by reference to an immense preponderance of boy candidates, and it was understood that the girls must be brought up to it. Extra time, and probably better teaching, aided by greater willingness on the part of the pupils, who had been made aware of their deficiency, were devoted to the unpopular and "useless" subject. In the next examination, out of the whole number of girls only three failed in it.

Other reasons for desiring a common standard, of a more subtle character, can scarcely be apprehended perhaps in their full force without personal experience. Probably only women who have laboured under it can understand the weight of discouragement produced by being perpetually told that, as women, nothing much is ever to be expected of them, and it is not worth their while to exert themselves—that they can write lively letters, full of graphic description and homely touches, but that anything like original research or profound learning is not for them to think of—that whatever they do they must not interest themselves, except in a second-hand and shallow way, in the pursuits of men, for in such pursuits they must always expect to fail. Women who have lived in the atmosphere produced by such teaching know how it stifles and chills; how hard it is to work courageously through it. Every effort to improve the education of women which assumes that they may, without reprehensible

ambition, study the same subjects as their brothers
and be measured by the same standards, does something towards lifting them out of the state of listless
despair of themselves into which so many fall. Supposing that the percentage of success attained by
women should be considerably less than that of men,
the sense of discouragement thus engendered would
be as nothing compared with the general self-distrust
produced by having it taken for granted that they
are by nature disqualified to stand the ordinary tests.
To make the discovery of individual incompetence
may be wholesomely humbling or stimulating, as
the case may be, but no one is the better for being
told, on mere arbitrary authority, that he belongs to
a weak and incapable class. And this, whatever
may be the intention, is said in effect by the offer
of any test of an exclusively female character. No
doubt there are university men whose opinion of
their own education is so low that they can hon-
estly propose a special standard for women with the
intention and expectation of its being better than
anything that has been known before, and an example
to be imitated in male examinations. But this idea
is so new and so bewildering to the outside world
that it is simply incomprehensible. The statement
of it is regarded as irony.

If it were otherwise—supposing that in the future
the relative positions of men and women as regards
Learning should be reversed—the arguments in favour
of common standards would be changed in their
application, but would remain substantially the same.

There would still be the same reasons for desiring that in all departments of study boys and girls, men and women, should walk together in the same paths. Why should they be separated? And the whole specializing system has a tendency, so far as its influence goes, to separate—to divide where union is most to be desired. The easy way in which it is often taken for granted that, as a matter of course, men care for men and women for women—that a certain *esprit de corps* is natural, if not positively commendable—must surely arise from a most inhuman way of looking at things. Conceive a family in which the brothers and sisters form rival *corps*, headed by the father and mother respectively! If on the small scale the spectacle is revolting, surely it ought to be no less so in the great human family. In the rebellion of the best instincts of human nature against such a theory, we have a security that it will never prevail. But sympathy may be checked even where it cannot be destroyed; and to put barriers in the way of companionship in the highest kinds of work and pleasure, is to carry out in the most effectual way the devices of the dividing spirit.

But when all has been said that can be, or that need be, said in favour of common standards, it may still be urged—All this is very well, but can you get them? What university is likely to open its degree-examinations to women? Would it not be well to try some judicious compromise?

To those who are aware that women have at this

moment free access to the degrees of several foreign universities, to say nothing of historic precedent, the idea of extending those of our own country is not so very startling. We see in the papers from time to time notices of ladies who have taken the degree of Bachelière-ès-Sciences, or Bachelière-ès-Lettres, at Paris, Lyons, or elsewhere; and three English ladies are now studying for the medical degree at the University of Zurich, without hindrance or restriction of any sort. In England the only university which could at present be reasonably asked to open its examinations to women is that of London. The condition of residence imposed by the old universities must exclude women until they are able, by means of a college of their own, to offer guarantees as to instruction and discipline similar to those which are required at Oxford and Cambridge. It is probable that within no very distant period the opportunity of complying with this essential condition will be within reach of women, and there is reason to hope that the examinations of the University of Cambridge may then be substantially, if not in name—and this last is a secondary consideration—as accessible to women as they are to men. But when this shall arrive, the wants of non-resident students will remain to be supplied; and here it is manifestly reasonable to look to the one English university which undertakes this particular work. The question has been before the University of London for some years, and a supplemental charter has been obtained, empowering the university to institute special examinations for women. The first step taken under this charter has been to draw up a scheme for a general or testing examination for women parallel with the matriculation examination for men; and by a curious coincidence, the subjects found specially appropriate to women are, with a few exceptions, precisely those which had already been laid down as specially proper for men. Greater option is given in the section for languages; for some inscrutable reason, one book of Euclid instead of four is considered enough for women, and by way of compensation physical geography is thrown in; English *Literature* is added to English language; and a choice is permitted between chemistry and botany. It will be observed that, except three books of Euclid, nothing which is considered good for men is *omitted,* the only substantial difference being that women are allowed greater freedom in selection. Whether this gift of liberty is better than guidance need not here be discussed. As to the level of attainment to be exacted, no official announcement has been made. It is confidently asserted that it will be in no way inferior, as regards difficulty, to the parallel matriculation examination; and as the subjects prescribed will, for a time at any rate, exclude ordinary half-educated women, it seems likely that the assertion will be justified.

Here then seems to be a fair case for compromise. To begin with, we have the authority of a university which is growing in public estimation and importance, which is recognised as the great examining board for all students whose circumstances preclude college life, and which year by year is acquiring more of that dignity which belongs only to age. Then, looking at the examination itself, and especially at the programme of subjects prescribed, it cannot be denied that it is admirably suited to the education of women in its present state of transition. Modern languages and English literature have their place by the side of classics, mathematics, and physical science. Taking the Schools Inquiry Commissioners as a guide—and there could scarcely be a better—we find that in their chapter on "Kinds of education desirable," their recommendations show a remarkable correspondence with the course laid down in the London programme. Some provision will no doubt be required to bring the requisite instruction within reach of women; but here we come upon one of the advantages of community of subjects, It is certain that as young men all over England are continually preparing for this examination, there must be people employed in teaching them, and by a little arrangement, the same teachers may be made available for their sisters. One of the benefits contingent on the use of such an examination is, that it may lead to the extension of good teaching. It is, of course, also possible that women may become the prey of the crammers, but probably not at all to the same extent as their brothers—the inducement to an unstudious woman to go through an examination merely for the sake of a pass being comparatively small. The matriculation examination is taken up by a large proportion of male students as their one and final test, and as such it will no doubt be made immediate use of by women.* If it should be found that the machinery works well, that the demand which has been alleged on the part of women is real, and if the students, by passing creditably this first stage, establish their claim to the complete university course, there is little doubt that it will ultimately be acknowledged. The step which has already been taken may be regarded as a tentative effort in the right direction, and public opinion is not likely to permit backsliding.

---

* It is estimated that nearly one-half of the undergraduates go no farther than matriculation. Taking the year 1865 as a specimen, it appears there were 616 candidates for matriculation and only 309 for the degree of Bachelor in the various faculties. The average age of candidates for matriculation has varied from seventeen years and eleven months to twenty years and ten months. In the years 1863-64-65 it was over twenty years.

Home and the Higher Education.

[The following paper contains the substance, with some alterations and additions, of an address given at the Annual Meeting of the Birmingham Higher Education Association, February 21, 1878.]

BEFORE entering upon any of the matters which more particularly claim our attention at such a meeting as this, I wish to offer my thanks to the Association for the opportunity and the inducement given to me to make acquaintance with its work. It seems very desirable that the labourers in various parts of the educational field should be cognisant of each other's work, the objects sought and the methods employed, the experiments set on foot, the successes and the failures, that we may learn from each other, and acquire something like a common stock of experience. For those who are chiefly occupied at what may be called a somewhat central position, it is a great gain to know, not only in the imperfect way that things are picked up from notices in the newspapers, but thoroughly, by close inspection, the details of important educational enterprises in various parts of the country; and I feel that I have added substantially to my own small stock of useful knowledge by studying the Reports of this Association. Feeling this, it has occurred to me that there might be some reciprocity in the matter, and that it might not be useless for me to state very briefly my impression as to the work going on in Birmingham. Putting it in the briefest form, I should say that the quality appears to me to be better than the quantity. I notice with pleasure the solid character of the subjects taken up—as *e.g.*, Latin, Greek, Algebra, Geometry, Trigonometry—and the favourable reports of the teachers on the progress made, and I confess that, for my own part, I would rather, in the interests of sound education, hear of small classes of real students, who genuinely respond to thorough teaching, than of large audiences flocking to popular lectures, listening with interest for the moment, and going away with some " general ideas" perhaps, but without having really mastered any part of what has been put before them. Still, while recognising the excellent quality of the work, and the value of quality as compared to quantity, one cannot but feel that in this great town the number of students might have been expected to be larger. It is evident that great zeal has been shown in providing the means of cultivation, but it does not appear that the young people of the place have, in any considerable number, shown a corresponding zeal in the use of the means.

Such an observation suggests inquiry as to the causes of the apparent apathy, which I am afraid is by no means confined to Birmingham, and I shall ask you presently to consider whether one of these causes may not consist in some errors in our general domestic policy—some mistakes in our internal family arrangements—and whether it might be possible to institute some not too revolutionary changes, which, on the part of the home, might from within meet half-way the efforts from without of this and kindred associations. If in dealing with such a subject what I have to say must be of a very simple and homely nature, I shall beg to be forgiven for the sake of the practical bearing which will, I hope, be found in any observations or suggestions that I may venture to make.

Before, however, going further, I wish to make one or two remarks on some points as to the classes and examinations held at Birmingham, regarded in connexion with the general provision of higher education for the upper and middle classes of this country.

I observe that considerable prominence has been given to the agency of the Cambridge Higher Local Examinations, and that classes have been organised with a special view to these Examinations, as well as, I am glad to see, for preparation for the London University Examinations.

I observe further, that while a good many of the ladies who have attended classes have obtained a Higher Local Certificate, the young men have declined to present themselves for that Examination; the explanation, suggested by your Committee in their Report for last year, being that the standard is too high for them. This might lead a bystander to the conclusion—agreeably flattering to women—that at Birmingham women are better educated than men.

It is not likely, however, that any one who knows a little of the general state of the higher education of women will rashly accept such a conclusion. For myself, being perhaps of a suspicious turn, I was not prepared to believe the flattering tale without investigation, and I find on inquiry that, as might have been expected, there is another explanation, *i.e.*, that the ladies who have taken these examinations are not in quite the same circumstances as the young men who have kept aloof from them—that they are not young women in business, having only their evenings and holidays unemployed, but for the most part, either governesses, whose daily work turns upon examination subjects, or ladies of leisure, the sisters of men who are, or might be, University graduates. It appears, therefore, that what has been done in these examinations ought rather to be regarded as a stepping-stone to higher things, than as a permanent resting-place. I cannot be satisfied for women to accept, and I do not believe that they will accept, permanently, a lower standing in the educational world than that of men, and I would invite the ladies who have done well in the Higher Local Examinations, to take a step forward, and occupy their natural place by the side of their brothers.

A few years ago such an appeal would have been manifestly futile. It would have been answered, with indisputable force—" All the Universities are closed to women. However much they may desire an education corresponding with that of their brothers, and however ready they may be to comply with all the conditions of a University course, the opportunity is denied them. Nothing at all parallel with the University education of men, is within reach of women."

Some years ago, as I have said, this would have been unanswerable. But things have happily changed. One great University, that of London, is, as we all know, at this moment taking the necessary steps for extending all its Degrees, just as they are, to women, and I suppose that in the course of this year the way will be perfectly open. This is a boon for which those who are interested in education are deeply indebted to the wise and courageous members of the University who have taken up the question, fought our battle, and carried it through to a successful issue. I hope that women will pay their share of the debt of gratitude in the most practical form, by entering in large numbers on the path thrown open to them, and I feel the more sanguine as to the place that Birmingham may be expected to take in this forward march, as this Association has already had experience in carrying on classes for preparation for the London Examinations, and it is abundantly evident that there will be the most cordial readiness to provide all that is needed for women in this direction. With regard to the establishment of a Local College, as suggested in the Report that we have just heard, it appears to me that steps towards it have already been taken by the formation of classes of adult students, and I see no reason why this course should not be continued, on, as we hope, an increasing scale, postponing any decision as to the form that further developments may take, until a considerable body of students has been gathered and larger experience gained.

A hope has been expressed, in which we must all concur, that before long Oxford and Cambridge may follow the example of the University of London, and open their Degrees also to women. There are many who hold that Degrees conferred like those of the University of London on the results of examinations, without conditions as to a course of instruction and discipline, fail to recognise an essential part of the best University education. Those of us who take this view must labour and hope for the admission of women, under fit conditions, to the high privileges of our old Universities. I cannot myself expect that so great a step as the formal opening of Oxford and Cambridge Degrees will be taken just yet, but in the meantime we must thankfully acknowledge the warm sympathy that has been shown, and the advances in this direction that have been already made. By the friendly aid of members of the University of Cambridge, so generously and unfailingly afforded that we have learnt to rely upon it with confidence, it is now possible to offer a woman a Certificate precisely corresponding in substance with the Cambridge B.A. Degree. The Girton College Degree-Certificate—so called in order to indicate its distinctive character— is conferred on exactly similar conditions to those imposed on a Graduate of the University of Cambridge. In order to be a Cambridge B.A. it is necessary to reside for a prescribed period, either at a College or as an Unattached Student, under instruction and discipline, as well as to pass certain prescribed examinations. Similarly a candidate for a Girton Degree-Certificate is required to reside at the College for the period prescribed for regular undergraduates by the University, under instruction and discipline—the instruction being given by distinguished members of the University—and also to pass examinations in the same papers, at the same time and under the same Examiners, as those for undergraduates. The examinations are not held formally under the authority of the University. It is a favour on the part of the Examiners, and occasionally one may not see his way to taking part in it. In that case his papers are looked over by a colleague. The essential point of obtaining a judgment in accordance with the University standard is thus secured.

The case being thus, as I have stated, that women have now fairly put before them the opportunity of obtaining a real University education, it appears to me that claims are established on the public and on parents. I would put it as a public question, whether those who have to appoint teachers of girls, either in schools or families, ought to be permanently satisfied with any lower standard than they demand for the teachers of boys. I say *permanently*, for I am well aware that for some time it will be impossible for all the teachers that are wanted to produce any qualification equivalent to a University Degree, and I should be sorry to seem to forget that there are personal gifts of greater importance than a mere academical qualification. We need to be on our guard against attaching too high a value to Degrees and Certificates. But this applies to both men and women. All that I urge is, that where it would be said, as in the case of masterships in the great schools for boys, that anyone not a graduate could scarcely be thought of, we should at least look forward to saying the same thing as to a mistress-ship —that it should not be said that a teacher of boys must of course have a Degree, but for a teacher of girls a Higher Local Certificate will do.

To parents also I would appeal, and would ask them to recognise the simple fact that their daughters, no less than their sons, need all that a complete and thorough education can do for them, and that where it would be a matter of course to send a boy to the University, it should be equally a matter of course to do as much for a girl. I know that here the difficulty will often arise, that whereas a clever boy may be sent to the University by the help of the Scholarship which he is sure to win, very little assistance of this kind is provided for women. The difficulty is real, but I think not insuperable. If time allowed, I believe it could be shown that even on purely commercial principles, to give a girl a University education is not a bad investment of capital, but I must not enter upon detail and will say no more on this point. I am afraid, indeed, that in speaking at all of such education as involves residence in College, I may seem to have wandered away from the specific business of this meeting, and also from the point which I began by proposing to bring specially under consideration, that of the organisation of home life with a view to the promotion of higher education. But I venture to think that what I have urged bears, not remotely, on our immediate business. I believe that though comparatively few women may be able to go to a distance for their education, these few will exercise an important influence on those who are left at home, and that the College life may re-act upon home life, and aid in producing just those modifications which are needed in order to bring it into happier relations with the circumstances of modern society. Here, indeed, I feel that I tread on dangerous ground. The mere suggestion that our sacred, time-honoured, happy English homes can have anything to learn from such an upstart, new-fangled institution as a College for women, must, I fear, be felt to be an audacity, if not an outrage. But there are times and places at which audacious things may be said. Birmingham is perhaps not an unsuitable place, and I hope it may prove that the present is not an unsuitable occasion, when I explain in what sense I regard the influence of the College on the home as likely to be beneficial. I must emphatically disclaim at the outset, any desire to turn homes upside down, putting the young people in the first place, and making the comfort and convenience of the parents subordinate to that of the children. Such a subversion of the fit order of things is far from being the object in view. I must premise also that I should be very sorry, if in anything I may have to say, there should be found the least semblance of a charge against parents of harshness or severity. On the contrary, I suppose, there never was a time when young people were made so much of, so petted and fussed over, one may say, as they are now. If we listen to schoolmasters and mistresses and college tutors, we hear far more of laxity of home discipline, and of excessive anxiety on the part of parents for the health and comfort and pleasure of their children, than of any tendency to harshness. But the misfortune is, that the kindly indulgence and the sacrifices that parents are willing to make, are so much in the direction of luxury and amusement—the piling up of enjoyment—and so little concern is shown comparatively for higher interests. A College, on the other hand, by the mere fact of its existence, asserts the claims of the higher life, and undertakes to provide for them. It is from this point of view, as dealing with the needs of our higher nature, that I venture to hope for some good results from a more general familiarity with College life. My idea is that there are certain principles, if I may so call them, underlying and governing the organisation of a College; that the same principles, with obvious limitations, ought to underlie and govern the organisation of a household of young people; that they are often forgotten or put aside in our ordinary home arrangements, and that therefore a salient example of their application may, without being minutely followed, be of use in calling attention to them, and suggesting attempts to carry them out in varying forms, according to varying circumstances. What these principles are, I would state briefly thus: that the strengthening and development of character by a discipline combining subordination to rule with a considerable amount of self-government, is one of the main objects to be kept in view by those who are responsible for the direction of the young during the intermediate stage between boyhood or girlhood and manhood or womanhood; and further—that the strengthening of the mind by studies of a bracing nature, and its enrichment by the acquisition of knowledge, are among the *duties* of life, and that therefore devotion to study, within reasonable limits, is not an abnormal thing, to be admired, or wondered at, or tolerated, or condemned, as our prejudices may dictate, but simply to be expected, as a matter of course, from any well-conducted young person. Acting upon these principles, a system of discipline is established, laying down certain general rules which must be obeyed, but at the same time throwing upon the students much of the responsibility of self-guidance; allowing, within necessary limits, much freedom in the choice of friends and companions, and in such matters as *e.g.* the management of health, relying upon the student's own good sense and self-control in the place of minute direction from above. Similarly as to studies—the best teaching is provided, and advice is at hand, but much latitude of choice is allowed both as to subjects and the apportionment of time, the arrangement of the general daily routine simply securing that whatever the study may be, it can be carried on under such conditions as shall make it most wholesome and fruitful. In a College, as is well known, a student has the inestimable advantage of being free from disturbance, able, not only to read in peace, but to "think things out"— to carry on sustained thought without liability to the worry and distraction of casual interruption. This great boon—the power of being alone—is perhaps the most precious distinctive feature of College life, as compared with that of an ordinary family. But a College supplies also the stimulus of sympathy and companionship, and this, not only in study, but in healthy physical sports. This last is an advantage we cannot afford to despise, looking upon it as an aid towards the development of a vigorous *physique*, the sound body fit for the habitation of the sound mind.

Now, how far is all this applicable to young people living at home? I believe that many of the advantages of a College might, in a greater or less degree, be attainable in a well ordered home, if only parents, and especially mothers, will give their earnest attention to the solution of the problem before them; and, above all, if they will give the reins to their imaginations, allowing themselves to picture a domestic interior somewhat different to what we see every day—a development of the family ideal which shall make room for, and even cherish, individuality. Such an expansion, by the mere fact of its allowing free play to individual tastes and energies, might do much to remove the jars and discords which too often mar the full flow of family harmony. Parents do not seem always to realise what is coming upon them when their young people leave school for good; no longer children at home for the holidays, but young men and women entering upon the business of life—a new element, requiring a new place to be made for it. Young men are, no doubt, to a great extent provided for. They are put into a business which takes them out of the house all day, and employs the largest part of their time, and the great point of regular systematic occupation is thus secured. But as to girls, it is often taken for granted that they will shake into their places, whether there is a place for them or not—and that they will find something to do; or, in other words, that they will invent a scheme of life for themselves and stick to it, without help or guidance. Surely this is expecting from them what is beyond their years. In an admirable work on education lately published—"The Action of Examinations," by Rev. H. Latham—a passage occurs which bears so aptly on this point that I take leave to quote it. "Self-direction," says Mr. Latham, "is a quality which is not expected early in life; youths, we know, even though they may be ready to apply themselves to work when it is given them, can rarely find work for themselves and set themselves to it." This is the view of an experienced College tutor as to young men; why should we expect young women to be different? Experience, I believe, testifies that in this respect they are very much alike. It is not so much that youth fails in inventiveness. It is common enough for girls, on leaving school—supposing that they have been at a good school, and have had their minds awakened and stirred—to draw up very neat and elaborate plans for carrying on their studies at home. They begin, perhaps, full of ardour and hope, but the end is most often disappointment and failure. They break down, partly from missing the stimulus of habit and companionship, partly from the want of support and encouragement from their superiors. It may be rejoined, perhaps, that they started on a wrong tack; that instead of aiming at self-improvement, they ought to have tried to make themselves useful. It is doubtful whether they would prosper better in this direction. In many parts of the country, girls are taken from school very early, even as early as sixteen, expressly on the theory that they are to be useful at home, and this sounds reasonable enough. It sounds well, when we hear that a girl is to be her mother's right hand, and so on. But before we can be sure that it is as good as it sounds, we want to know more exactly of what use she is to be at home, and whether her mother wants a right hand. For if the mother has already two very good hands of her own, it may be that another is not wanted, and that being superfluous, it may grow weak and flaccid from insufficient exercise. I do not mean to assert that usefulness at home is a

mere fiction. What I urge is, that before household
duty is fixed upon as a girl's sole function, there
should be serious consideration as to whether there
is enough of it adequately to occupy and develop her
energies, and also whether a long period, perhaps
many years, exclusively devoted to it, is likely to be
the best preparation for any future that may be in
store for her. If such a case can be made out, then,
regarding the household as a place of business, there
may be the same sort of reason for giving a girl a
place in it that there is for putting a boy into an
office. Only, it should be done with as much deliberation and purpose in the one case as in the other.
There may be some analogy too, even in details. I
understand that when a youth goes into an office, he
is not expected to wait about all day, on the chance
of something turning up. He is not told that he will
find something to do, if he really wishes it, or that
he is to look about him and watch for opportunities
of making himself useful. He has his appointed
post, his own desk and his stool, and regular work cut
out for him. And when he has learnt the business,
he receives a salary, and is recognised as doing work
of appreciable importance. As a rule, there is not
the same order in the conduct of household business,
so far as the young ladies are concerned. It is
usual for the whole family to congregate in one room,
each being alike the victim of every interruption,
every one carrying on her individual occupation in
suspense, so to speak, liable at any moment to be
called off from it for something else, trifling or

important, as the case may be. Naturally enough, these half occupied people prey upon each other.

Gaiety is of course, to many, the most absorbing pursuit, but there are besides, various pernicious practices by which even very quiet people manage to get rid of a great deal of time. One, largely prevalent, called " dropping in," which means paying little insignificant visits at all hours of the day, is specially noxious. There used to be another terrible institution, known as " spending the day," which meant going to your neighbour's house at one o'clock and staying till ten, with nothing to do for the whole of those nine hours but to sit and chat, with perhaps a bit of fancy work in your hand. This is, I believe, dying out, but there still remains the custom of receiving visitors for several days or weeks, during which they are expected to be constantly entertained from morning till night. The process is wearisome enough for the guests, and terribly demoralising to the poor hostesses, who conceive themselves obliged by hospitality to make this sacrifice of the order and continuity of their daily occupations. By way of indemnity they return the visits, thus securing to themselves a double loss. Unfortunately, the young people belonging to circles in which these customs prevail, are almost powerless against them. They can scarcely make any effectual resistance without giving offence, or even pain, and incurring the reproach of being unsociable and illnatured. Attempts to make a stand against wholesale interruptions are pretty sure to be met by expressions of surprise and

Questions relating to Women
[1878

regret, if not actual remonstrance. It is really
pathetic to hear of the efforts that well-disposed
young women will make to do something better with
their lives; how they will join an Essay Society, or
a society for the encouragement of Home Study, or
a Reading Society—I have heard of one which com-
pels its members under penalties to read for a certain
time every day; these things being resorted to, not
only as a defence against their own idleness and
desultoriness, but also as something of the nature of
"an outward and visible sign," something which can
be held up to relations and friends as a plea for the
concession of a little slice of quiet time.

If the faithfulness of this picture is admitted, as I
think it will be, at least in part, and allowing for
exceptions, it may still be said, How can it be helped?
A mother cannot be running after her girls all day,
setting them to work at every turn; what can she
do?—what have you to suggest? I would ask her to
remember the first principle: that the young need a
framework within which to use their reasonable
liberty, and also that other principle, that mental
culture is a duty, and not a mere fancy or indulgence.
I believe that if these principles are laid to heart,
modes of applying them will be found, but I will
venture, with submission, to throw out one or two
practical hints as to details. Would it be possible
for the mistress of a household, when planning her
daughter's place in it, to fix upon certain definite
service to be expected from her, be it much or little,
and having laid down what is required, to leave it to

154

the daughter's discretion, subject of course to the general convenience, to do it at her own time, it being understood that when this regular work is done, the rest of her time is at her own disposal? Or, if this is thought impracticable, could certain hours be fixed upon—something corresponding to a man's office hours—and set apart for domestic or social claims, and the rest be considered her own? If this could be arranged, then I would ask further, that if she chooses to give her own time to study, it may be treated with so much respect as that it shall be possible to pursue it in quiet and comfort, not in the midst of the family circle—and that a certain warmth of approval may accompany it, so that the student may go to it with an untroubled conscience. I would lay stress on this point of the untroubled conscience, because I am afraid that much of women's work of this sort is done with an uneasy mind, a haunting doubt as to whether they are not selfishly pleasing or benefiting themselves, when they ought perhaps to be doing something for other people. It is easy to see how such questionings must take the heart out of the work, making it dull and spiritless, even if there be no grave injury done to the moral sense.

I have spoken of the conditions of home life chiefly as they affect the women who are expected to find in it their sphere, but I wish to add a word with reference to the young men whom this Association specially desires to aid. I am afraid that in doing so I may seem to be taking a leaf out of the book of those great statesmen and orators, who, when asked to speak at such a meeting as this, deliver a long discourse entirely occupied with the interests of boys or men, and, at the end, throw in a word or two for women, just to show that they are aware of their existence and have a friendly feeling for them. Women may be tempted sometimes to feel a little aggrieved at this sort of treatment, but it seems to me only natural. The orator speaks of what he knows, and there is generally this compensation, that though he may have been only thinking of men, his instructive utterances are equally applicable to women, who need feel no scruple in profiting by them. Similarly, though I have spoken primarily of what I know best, I venture to hope that what I have said will be found to be, in principle, susceptible of a wider application. I have urged the need of guidance, of sympathy, of encouragement, and of such recognition of the worth of intellectual and spiritual culture as shall lead to the greatest facilities being given for its pursuit in the details of domestic arrangements. Surely all this applies to young men as well as to women. They too, are human, they need the warm breath of social and domestic approval to counteract the chilling influences which surround us all, and against which we have to maintain a continual struggle. They, too, need to be reminded that it is not the whole duty of men to produce money, any more than it is of women to distribute it—that there is a higher life, always liable to be choked by the cares and the pleasures of the material, visible world around us. Does not the apathy that we have to contend with arise mainly from a too exclusive devotion to comfort and pleasure? and is not this lower sort of life, with its petty aspirations and aims, too often fostered and encouraged by the low tone of social and domestic opinion? We do not, it seems to me, sufficiently estimate the immense weight of social and domestic opinion, or fully realise all that we should gain if this vast force could be brought to pronounce decisively on the side of the higher life, by recognising the duty of mental and spiritual cultivation for both men and women. Hitherto it has often been cold and indifferent, when not positively hostile. Let us hope that through the united efforts, in all parts of the country, of such missionaries of culture as the founders of this Association, social and domestic opinion may be gradually leavened and converted, or—to put it in another form—the social and domestic conscience enlightened and stimulated. To contribute towards the realisation of this aim, though it may sound somewhat vague, is to my mind of deeper and wider import than any of the details of effort, though these are necessary and must not be neglected. I can but congratulate the people of Birmingham on having among them this Association, so well deserving of their confidence, living and working and expressing emphatically before the world their sense of the value of culture. And I venture to predict, as well as warmly to wish for the Association, a future worthy of the devotion and the public spirit which led to its formation, and with which it has been carried on.

Women in the Universities of England and Scotland.

[*Published at Cambridge, May*, 1896].

In the recent controversy on the proposed admission of women to Oxford and Cambridge Degrees, a notable feature has been the apparent absence of knowledge in regard to a movement which, having been in progress for some fifty years, has now reached a somewhat advanced stage. The present proposals have been treated as portending a sudden revolution; speculation as to what might happen in certain contingencies has taken the place of calm consideration of existing facts; much anxiety has been expressed as to the dangers of mixed universities, of co-education, of a hasty assimilation of the education of women to that of men; and it has been urged that, in so serious a matter, it is most necessary to guard against precipitate action, which might imperil interests of the gravest importance. Of the many successive tentative steps, quietly and cautiously taken, which have led up to the present position, but little appears to be known, and thus the guidance which might be obtained from the lessons of experience has not been sought. Under these circumstances I have thought that it might be helpful, and of some interest, to present in chronological order such stages as can be definitely marked in the progress of the movement, and to note points which may have special bearing on questions now under discussion. I propose to confine my statement to England and Scotland, leaving on one side any reference to important action taken elsewhere, partly for the sake of brevity, and partly on account of the large amount of time and labour required for searching out and verifying details spread over a long period and a wide field.

So far as the beginning of such a movement as we have in view can be assigned to any particular action, it may be traced to the first efforts for the establishment of women's Colleges in London. In 1848 the Governesses' Benevolent Institution made arrangements with " Professors of high talent and standing in society to open classes in all branches of female education," and having received permission to give to this branch of their work the name of Queen's College, started the institution at 67, Harley Street. In 1849 a similar institution was opened at 47, Bedford Square.

At that date even the name of ' College,' as associated with women, seemed to require apology. In an inaugural lecture given by Professor F. D. Maurice on March 29th, 1848, he says:

" It is proposed, immediately after Easter, to open a College in London for the education of females. The word ' College ' in this connexion has to English ears a novel and ambitious sound. I wish we could have found a simpler one which would have described our object as well. Since we have chosen this, we should take pains to explain the sense in which we use it; to show, if we can show truly, that we are not devising a scheme to realise some favourite theory, but are seeking, by humble and practical methods, to supply an acknowledged deficiency."

Even at that time such masculine studies as Latin and mathematics were held to be fit subjects for female education, and were included in the programme of the new College. Of one of these subjects Professor Maurice says:

"We have set down mathematics in our course of studies, knowing that we might thereby encounter the charge of giving a little learning, which is dangerous, but being ready to meet that charge in this case as in others. We are aware that our pupils are not likely to advance far in mathematics, but we believe that if they learn really what they do learn they will not have got what is dangerous, but what is safe. . . . . The least bit of knowledge that is knowledge must be good, and I cannot conceive that a young lady can feel her mind in a more dangerous state than it was because she has gained one truer glimpse into the conditions under which the world in which it has pleased God to place her actually exists."

Some years later, Greek was added to the curriculum. At Bedford College, Latin, Mathematics, and Natural Science have been taught continuously since 1849, and Greek from 1875 to the present time.

These Colleges, however, were only in a general sense pioneers in the movement for opening universities to women. They were self-contained, and there is no evidence that they aimed at being attached to any university. The first attempt to obtain the admission of a woman to membership of a university seems to have been made by Miss Jessie Meriton White, who in May 1856 addressed a letter to the Registrar of the University of London, inquiring whether a woman could "become a candidate for a diploma in medicine, if on presenting herself for examination she shall produce all the requisite certificates of character, capacity, and study from one of the institutions recognised by the London University." The opinion of Counsel having been taken, it was on July 9th, 1856, resolved by the Senate, "That Miss J. M. White be informed that the Senate, acting upon the opinion of its legal adviser, does not consider itself empowered to admit females as candidates for degrees."

The question was again brought before the Senate by an application in 1862 from Miss Elizabeth Garrett, requesting to be admitted as a candidate at the next Matriculation examination, whereupon it was resolved, "That the Senate, as at present advised, sees no reason to doubt the validity of the opinion given by Mr. Tomlinson, July 9th, 1856, as to the admissibility of females to the examinations of the University." On the receipt of this reply, Mr. Newson Garrett, having been informed that the University was about to apply for a new Charter, presented a memorial to the Senate, supported by persons of weight and influence, in which it was suggested that "the technical legal objection, which appears to be the only obstacle to the admission of women, may be removed by the insertion of a clause expressly providing for the extension to women of the privileges of the University." On May 7th it was moved by the Vice-Chancellor, Mr. Grote, and seconded by the Right Hon. R. Lowe, M.P., "That the Senate will endeavour, as far as their powers reach, to obtain a modification of the Charter, rendering female students admissible to the degrees and honours of the University of London on the same conditions of examination as male students, but not rendering them admissible to become members of Convocation." The motion was lost by the casting vote of the Chancellor.

*　　*　　*　　*

The effort which had been made was not however fruitless. Those who were interested in the matter had been brought together, and on Oct. 23rd, 1862, a Committee was formed for obtaining the admission of women to university examinations. It had been represented that the University of London objected to being made a *corpus vile* on which all experiments were to be tried, and that any action taken at Oxford or Cambridge in favour of the claims of women would be a valuable encouragement to the younger University. The Committee accordingly made it their first business to work for the admission of girls to the Local Examinations, the only step which at that time the older universities could reasonably be asked to take on behalf of women. They entered into communication with the local committees, and a member of one of them, Mr. Acland, gave valuable advice. He told us that the secret of his success in originating, conjointly with Dr. Temple, the Oxford Local Examinations, was that they had, as a preliminary step, held an examination similar to that which they desired to see established by the University— "we showed at Exeter that our ideas could march." Mr. Acland wrote from Oxford on May 8th, 1863:

"I think it might be worth while to form a Committee in London or elsewhere which would guarantee *all expenses*, including payment *pro ratâ* to examiners for additional work, and then to apply to the Delegates for leave to print off some additional examination papers (that must be done here of course to secure secrecy), and for leave to make a private arrangement with the examiners to look over the answers and to receive their report. I am strongly of opinion that the way to get an old institution to take up a matter is to prove its feasibility without committing the institution."

The advice was acted upon, and an application was addressed to Cambridge, to which the following reply, from the Secretary of the Local Examinations Syndicate, was received:

"UNIVERSITY LOCAL EXAMINATIONS. . . *Oct. 23rd*, 1863. —The Syndicate for conducting the above examinations direct me to reply to your letter of Sept. 26th. They have agreed to have printed the extra copies of the examination papers, and to direct their examiner in London to give these out to some responsible person appointed by your Committee on each occasion after he shall have given them out to the boys. The Syndicate decline to *order* the examiners in the various subjects to look over the answers of the girls, but leave it to your Committee to make what arrangements you please with the examiners.

"I have given Mr. Tomkinson [Hon. Sec. to the London Local Committee for boys] an account of this decision.

"I shall be glad to receive the numbers of your students in each subject of examination, either directly from you or through Mr. Tomkinson when he sends in the number of the boys.

"I enclose a list of the examiners, and shall be glad to assist you in communicating with them, either by forwarding letters to them, or writing to them, or in any other way."

The Committee encouraged by this friendly response to their application, thereupon resolved, " That a private examination of girls be held, in accordance with the University Regulations, and simultaneously

with that of the boys, commencing Dec. 14th, 1863."
Schoolmistresses in London and the country were
invited to send in candidates, and ninety were entered
for examination. The university examiners gave
their cordial co-operation, and the experiment was
successful in two ways. It proved that the scheme
was perfectly workable as applied to girls, and it
showed that the more solid branches of female education needed encouragement and support. Out of forty
senior girls, six only passed, the remaining thirty-
four having failed in the preliminary arithmetic.

While these practical steps were being taken in
connection with Cambridge, the Committee were
also in correspondence with the Secretary of the
Oxford Local Examination Delegacy, but it was not
considered advisable to make any formal application
to the University at that time.

In the Michaelmas Term 1864 the following memorial was addressed to the Vice-Chancellor and Senate
of the University of Cambridge :

"Gentlemen,—As being officially engaged in or connected
with female education, we beg respectfully to call your attention
to the existing want of some publicly recognised examination
for girls. We believe that this want could in no way be better
supplied than by the extension to girls of the University Local
Examinations. The representations by which the Universities
were induced to accord these advantages to boys apply with
at least equal force to girls, and it appears to us that no valid
objection can be urged against the admission of girls to similar
benefits.

"We venture therefore earnestly to request that you will be
pleased to give your sanction to a measure by which the usefulness of the scheme for Local Examinations may be largely
extended."

Women in the Universities

The memorial received 999 signatures and was accompanied by a list of influential supporters interested in, though not professionally connected with, the education of girls. On Nov. 24th a Syndicate was appointed " to consider whether any system of examinations, similar to that established by Grace of the Senate, February 11th, 1858, for boys, may be extended to girls," and in February 1865 they presented their report, from which the following extracts are taken:

" They have carefully considered the various points in which the scheme of the Local Examinations for boys is applicable to girls, and any modification which might be necessary to adapt it to the latter class. . . . The subjects for examination for boys are the English Language and Literature, History, Geography, the Greek, Latin, French, and German Languages, Arithmetic, Mathematics, Natural Philosophy, some branches of Natural Science, Drawing, and the Elements of Music. The Syndicate by their regulations have made some of these subjects obligatory and others optional. . . . The same course might be adopted with regard to girls, and the same subjects retained at the discretion of the Syndicate. The Syndicate consider it quite inexpedient to introduce others which belong exclusively to female education."

As regards details of management the Syndicate are cautious and conservative. After remarking that the boys' examinations are held at different local centres under the superintendence of examiners appointed by the Syndicate, the arrangements for holding them being made by local committees or secretaries, they suggest that " a similar plan might be adopted with regard to examinations for girls, the committees in such cases being composed of ladies, and care being taken to prevent undue publicity or intrusion." They recommend that neither the names of the candidates nor any class-lists be published.

The report was discussed in the Arts School on March 2nd, and on March 9th the vote was taken. The measure was carried by fifty-five votes to fifty-one. Thus, probably with but little prevision of the far-reaching consequences of its action, the Senate of the University of Cambridge took its first step in recognition of duties and responsibilities in regard to the higher education of women. The scheme was enacted for three years only, but on the expiration of that period no opposition was offered to its renewal. It may be worthy of note that concurrently with the admission of girls there was a marked increase in the numbers of male candidates. In 1863, the year of the informal examination of girls, 629 boys were entered; in 1864 there were 844; and in 1865, the year in which the admission of girls was formally authorised, the number rose to 1217.

Early in 1865 an application for the extension of the Oxford Examinations was laid before the Hebdomadal Council, with the result that it was decided to take no steps upon it.

The Local Examinations of the University of Durham were opened to girls in 1866.

In the meantime our friends in the University of London were not idle. The question of examinations for women was kept in view by repeated discussions in Convocation, and in June 1866 it was again brought before the Senate. It was moved by Dr. Storrar, Chairman of Convocation:

"That it is desirable to establish in the University an examination for women special in its nature, and that it be referred to the Committee on Examinations in Arts, Science, and Laws to prepare a scheme for such an examination for the consideration of the Senate."

An amendment, moved by Mr. Grote, "That the words 'special in its nature' be omitted from the motion," having been lost, the original motion was carried, and it was further resolved "that the opinion of the Law Officers of the Crown be taken as to the power of the Senate, under the provision of the Charter, to institute a special examination for women." In the case laid before the Law Officers it is stated that—

"It has been proposed by Convocation that a Special Examination for women shall be instituted by the University, *not* with the view of inaugurating an academical course which should lead to graduation in one or other of the Faculties in which degrees are granted by it, but for the purpose of rewarding by certificates of proficiency (according to the provisions of Clause 41 of the Charter, which has not hitherto been acted on) such female candidates as shall satisfactorily pass an examination special in its nature, but not on the whole less difficult than the existing matriculation examination, so that such certificates of proficiency may serve as attestations that the candidates who obtain them have received a thoroughly good general education."

The Opinion given was to the following effect:

"The same reasons and arguments which would prevent examinations for, and the conferring of degrees upon, women seem to us to apply equally to examinations for, and the granting of, certificates for women.

"We do not see that any distinction can properly be drawn between the two cases; and although the effect practically of a mere certificate is no doubt very different to that of a degree, we are of opinion that the examination of, and granting certificates to, women is not within the scope of, or authorised by, the present Charter of the University."

Under these circumstances it was decided to apply for a Supplemental Charter enabling the University to establish special examinations for women, and this having been obtained, a scheme was drawn up providing a General Examination on the lines of the Matriculation Examination, with some modifications, and offering also certificates of higher proficiency in fourteen different subjects. The first General Examination was held in May 1869.

While the advocates of a separate curriculum were thus carrying out their views in the University of London, other proceedings were taken elsewhere.

Valuable as was the work of the Local Examinations in improving the schools, it was abundantly evident that the most serious deficiency in regard to the higher education of women was one which they could not meet. The investigations of the Schools Inquiry Commission of 1864 brought into view the absence of any satisfactory provision for women's education beyond the school period. The Assistant Commissioners appointed to selected districts, one after another called attention to this defect; but by none, perhaps, was the deficiency so keenly felt as by the more enlightened and zealous schoolmistresses, who were constantly subjected to the disappointment of finding that the high aims and aspirations which had been kindled during school life were stifled or starved in later years. In a memorial from teachers of girls to the Schools Inquiry Commissioners, the belief was expressed that " opportunities of undergoing a course of instruction and discipline adapted to advanced students, combined with examinations testing and attesting the quality of the education received" would be eagerly welcomed. These various representations were not unheeded. After much consideration and discussion, a project was launched for the establishment of a College "designed to hold in relation to girl's schools and home teaching a position analogous to that occupied by the universities towards the public schools for boys." Certain fundamental principles having been agreed upon, a Committee was formed to carry out the scheme. This Committee met for the first time on Dec. 5th, 1867, and in October 1869 the College was opened in a hired house at Hitchin, under the direction of Mrs. Manning, a member of the Committee, who had consented to reside as Mistress during the first term. The co-operation of competent lecturers having been secured, the small band of students set to work, beginning with the somewhat humble task of preparing for the Previous Examination. In November 1870 the Committee applied to the Council of the Senate of the University of Cambridge for permission to make use of the papers to be issued for the then approaching Previous Examination, and to make a private arrangement with the examiners for looking over and reporting upon the answers, and for conducting the *viva voce* part of the examination. A reply was received to the effect that the Council did not consider it within their province to give such permission, but they did not disapprove of such a private arrangement being made with the examiners, if practicable. The examiners having consented to undertake the work, five students were examined, and the following report was received:

"I certify that the undermentioned students of Hitchin College were examined by the examiners for the Previous Examination in the subjects appointed for that examination, and that Miss Cook, Miss Lumsden, Miss Townsend, and Miss Woodhead attained the standard required for a First Class, and Miss Gibson that required for a Second Class, and also that Miss Gibson and Miss Woodhead were examined in the Additional Subjects and approved.

"(Signed)

"J. W. CARTMELL,
"*Senior Examiner.*
"CAMBRIDGE, *Dec.* 14*th*, 1870."

Two years later Miss Woodhead passed the examination for the Mathematical Tripos, and Miss Cook and Miss Lumsden that for the Classical Tripos. By the generous aid of the examiners, this informal, but none the less strictly regular, system of examinations was continued in subsequent years, both for the Ordinary Degree and for various Triposes. In 1872 the College was incorporated under the name of Girton College, and in 1873 it was removed to a building of its own at Cambridge.

Women in the Universities

The founders of Girton College were not alone in their endeavours to obtain the assistance of the University of Cambridge in supplying the deficiencies in the higher education of women. In March 1868 a draft memorial to the University asking for advanced examinations for women was forwarded to the above mentioned Committee for obtaining the admission of women to university examinations. The draft having been considered, it was resolved:

> "That this Committee, believing that the distinctive advantage of the Cambridge University Local Examinations consists in their offering a common standard to boys and girls, and that the institution of independent schemes of examination for women exclusively, tends to keep down the level of female education, cannot take part in the proposed memorial to the University of Cambridge for advanced examinations for women above the age of eighteen."

The memorial was presented and favourably received; and examinations for women above eighteen years of age were instituted in 1869. With regard to this step it may be observed that, however opinions may differ as to the expediency of separate examinations, it may be looked upon as a mark of the interest taken by the University in the education of women. The same may be said of similar action taken later at Oxford and elsewhere. Lectures, having the women's examinations in view, were started at Cambridge in January 1870; and in October 1871, in consequence of the demand from women at a distance to share the advantage of the lectures, a house for them was opened under the charge of Miss A. J. Clough. In October 1873, an Association for promoting the higher education of women in Cambridge was formed to carry on and develope the lectures for women. Newnham Hall was opened in 1875, and subsequently Newnham College was formed by the amalgamation of the Newnham Hall Company with the Association for promoting the higher education of women. Students were presented informally for Tripos examinations from 1874 onwards, without, however, its being made indispensable that they should have fulfilled the conditions imposed on undergraduates as regards the time limit and the preliminary examinations to be passed.

The Oxford and Cambridge Schools Examination Board, formed, in accordance with articles of agreement signed on November 8th, 1873, by representatives of the two Universities, admitted girls to its examinations from the outset. The Board examines such schools as have a regularly constituted governing body, or prepare a fair proportion of their boys for the Universities, or in any other way give evidence of providing an education of the highest grade, and it also examines for certificates, higher and lower. It examines girls under the same regulations as for boys, with four additional regulations, providing for the option of substituting Italian for Greek, and Music for Natural Philosophy (Mechanical Division), and of being examined in Drawing, and of passing the examination in two portions. The higher certificates confer exemption, under certain conditions, from the Cambridge Previous Examination and the Oxford Examination for Responsions.

The Oxford Local Examinations were opened to girls in 1870. A scheme of lectures and classes was set on foot by a committee of ladies in 1873. Examinations for women over eighteen were instituted in 1875. An Association for promoting the education of women in Oxford was founded in 1878, and in 1879 Lady Margaret Hall and Somerville Hall were opened for the reception of resident students.

To return to the University of London. After the inauguration of the Women's Examinations, proposals for alterations in the regulations were made from time to time, and in 1874, memorials were presented from Associations for improving the education of women in various parts of the country, expressing dissatisfaction with the existing system, and urging afresh the plea for degrees, one memorial in a contrary sense being also sent in. In 1877 a new phase of the question appeared. The Senate having expressed their readiness to exercise the powers given by the Russell Gurney Act, which would have enabled them to admit women to degrees in Medicine only, the proposed action was strongly disapproved by the Convocation of the University. A controversy ensued, happily closed by an agreement on both sides in favour of admitting women to degrees in all the faculties. I refrain from further details, and will quote instead a summary of the situation taken from a sketch of the Origin and History of the University, given in the Calendar:

"The experiment of offering encouragement for women to pursue a course of academic education was at first tried under limitations which somewhat impeded its success. Under the powers given in the Charter of 1867, women were not rendered admissible to the ordinary examinations, but two forms of certificate were offered to female students, the one of general, and the other of higher, proficiency. In the scheme for both examinations prominence was given to those subjects which it was presumed that women and their teachers would prefer. But the number availing themselves of this privilege was small, and the privilege itself was not highly valued. Moreover, it was found that the chief distinctions attained by women in these examinations were not gained in the special subjects, but in the classical languages and in science. It was urged by the teachers that women did not desire a scheme of instruction exclusively devised for their use, but would prefer to have access to the ordinary degrees and honours, and to be subject to the same tests of qualification which were imposed on other students.

"After much discussion the Senate and Convocation agreed to accept from the Crown in 1878 a Supplemental Charter, making every degree, honour, and prize awarded by the University accessible to students of both sexes on perfectly equal terms. The University of London was thus the first academical body in the United Kingdom to admit women as candidates for degrees. The record of the results which have followed this measure will be found in the statistical tables, and in the honours and distinctions which have since been won by female students."*

Early in 1880 a link was formed between Girton College and the University of Cambridge. On an application from the College, the Council of the Senate consented to exercise the power, conferred upon it by one of the College Articles of Association,

---

* The Supplemental Charter contained a provision that "no female graduate of the said University shall be a member of the Convocation of the said University unless and until such Convocation shall have passed a resolution that female graduates be admitted to Convocation." On January 17th, 1882, it was resolved by Convocation "that female graduates be admitted to Convocation."

of electing three representative members of the
College. The members first appointed were selected
in view of their eminence respectively in three great
branches of learning, Classics, Mathematics, and
Natural Science. This first formal recognition on
the part of the University of a women's College was
the more significant, as the College had been for six
years established within the University precincts,
and members of the Council had had opportunities
of judging for themselves of its working, both as
regards its own students and in relation to the
University.

The same year was marked by a generous recognition of the claim of women to University membership
in the Charter of the Victoria University, dated 20th
April 1880, in which it is declared that :

"The University shall have power to grant and confer all
such degrees and other distinctions as now or at any time hereafter can be granted and conferred by any other University in
our United Kingdom of Great Britain and Ireland to and on all
persons, male or female, who shall have pursued a regular course
of study in a College in the University, and shall submit themselves for examination."

In this year also a crisis in regard to the Degree
question arose at Cambridge. A student of Girton
College having been declared to have shown in the
Mathematical Tripos Examination proficiency equal
to that of the eighth Wrangler—at that early date,
a very high distinction—a large amount of public
attention and sympathy was aroused. The occasion
was seized for bringing the question of degrees for

women before the University. A memorial promoted by Mr. and Mrs. Aldis, of Newcastle-upon-Tyne, and signed by 8500 persons, set forth that "repeated instances of success on the part of students of Girton and Newnham Colleges in satisfying the examiners in various degree examinations at Cambridge, and notably an instance in connection with the last Mathematical Tripos, show that many women desire sound training in higher learning, and also desire to have the result of that training authoritatively tested and certified," and prayed that the Senate would "grant to properly qualified women the right of admission to the examinations for University degrees, and to the degrees conferred according to the result of such examinations."

This was followed by memorials:

(1) From the Executive Committee of Girton College, submitting that by an experimental process — particulars of which were given—" the practical working of degree examinations, as regards students of Girton College, has been sufficiently tested to justify the University in taking their case into serious consideration, with a view to their formal admission to the B.A. degree."

(2) From the Committee of the Association for promoting the higher education of women in Cambridge, also referring to the informal examinations, and stating that they would "welcome any arrangements by which the connection that has practically existed for some years between the University examinations and the academic instruction provided for

women in Cambridge, may be put on a more formal and stable footing."

(3) From 123 resident members of the Senate expressing their "general approval of the measure proposed by the Committee" of the Association for promoting the higher education of women in Cambridge.

A Syndicate having been appointed to consider these four memorials, they received in addition ten memorials from various educational bodies, and one from 567 non-resident members of the Senate. Of these, two asked generally for degrees; the remaining nine, including that from members of the Senate, asked for the B.A. degree only. The conclusions arrived at by the Syndicate are contained in the following paragraph of their report:

"The Syndicate share the desire of the memorialists that the advantage of academic training may be secured to women, and that the results of such training may be authoritatively tested and certified. For various reasons, however, they are not prepared to recommend that women should be admitted either to the degrees of the University generally or to the B.A. degree alone. They believe that the two objects above mentioned may be in a large measure attained, and great encouragement be given to the higher education of women, by the formal admission of female students to the Honour examinations of the University, together with an authoritative record of the results of their examination in published class lists. The advantages of allowing women to enter the General and Special Examinations for the Ordinary B.A. degree are less obvious, and the Syndicate abstain from making any recommendation on this head. They think that women admitted to the Honours examinations should be required to have fulfilled the same conditions of residence as are imposed on members of the University, and that they should either have given the same evidence of preliminary training by passing the Previous Examination, or one of the various substitutes already accepted for it, or else should have obtained an Honour certificate in the Higher Local Examination, with the condition of passing in certain specified groups. They propose that the University should grant to each successful candidate a certificate setting forth the conditions under which she has been admitted to the Tripos examinations and the standard to which she has attained."

Graces embodying the recommendations of the Syndicate passed the Senate on February 24th, 1881, and Graces providing for carrying out the details of the measure having subsequently passed without opposition, the scheme came into practical operation in June 1881.

In May 1882 the Board of Musical Studies presented a report, confirmed by the Senate on June 15th, recommending that women be allowed to present themselves for the University examinations for degrees in Music, on producing the required certificate of literary and scientific attainment, and that the Vice-Chancellor be authorised to grant certificates to those who should have passed the examinations for the degrees of Mus.Bac. and Mus.D. respectively.

At Oxford a statute was passed in 1884 opening to women Honour Moderations and the Final Honour Schools of Mathematics, Natural Science, and Modern History. In 1886 women were admitted to Responsions; in 1888 to the Final Honours School of Literae Humaniores; in 1890 to the Honour School of Jurisprudence and the Final Examination for B.Mus.; in 1893 to the Honour Schools of Theology and of

Oriental Studies, and the Examination for Mus.D.;
and in 1894 to the remaining examinations for the
B.A. degree. In 1886 St. Hugh's Hall was opened.
In 1893 the Association for promoting the education
of women in Oxford was formally recognised by the
University, by the appointment, as a member of its
Council, of a representative of the Hebdomadal
Council.

In 1887 the Cambridge examinations scheme
having been in operation for some years, it was held
that the time had arrived for inviting the University
to take a further step. A Committee was formed
for the purpose of promoting the admission of duly
qualified women to Cambridge degrees, and memorials were presented, including one signed by 842
members of the Senate. Counter memorials, signed
by 271 resident and 1360 non-resident members of
the Senate were also sent in, and on March 5th,
1888, the Council presented a report to the Senate,
containing the following statement:

"Having given careful consideration to the question, the
Council have decided not to propose the appointment of a
Syndicate to consider a change in the constitution of the University, which the majority of the Council do not believe to be in
itself desirable, and which must lead to much discussion and
controversy, when there is so clear an indication of the balance
of opinion among the memorialists who are members of the
Senate."

Commenting on the report, the above mentioned
Committee state that they

"are satisfied that the presentation of the memorials has
been of great service, by bringing the question under discussion,

and thus contributing towards the ripening of opinion. It is admitted that some of those who have on this occasion either opposed the movement or remained neutral have done so because they think the request inopportune rather than because they stand irrevocably pledged to resistance, while there are others who require more time for consideration. In view of the generous sympathy and support which the present effort has received, the Committee look forward with hope to ultimate success."

In 1895 another English University, that of Durham, became "mixed," a Supplementary Charter having been obtained enabling the University to grant degrees to women in all the faculties except Theology. It is gratifying to learn, on the authority of the Warden of the University, that the new departure has been warmly welcomed, both by the teaching staff and the undergraduates. The Principal of the Durham College of Science at Newcastle-on-Tyne, the classes of which have been mixed from its foundation in 1871, is of opinion that the women-students exercise an influence in the college which is entirely beneficent.

Passing now to Scotland, we find the University of Edinburgh taking the foremost place in opening its Local Examinations to girls in 1865. In 1869 an Association was formed for the University education of women, and arrangements were made with individual professors and lecturers for the holding of classes in rooms provided by the Association. In 1874 a certificate was instituted by the University, which was granted to students of the Association who were registered in the books of the University as having attended classes conducted by professors or lecturers whose teaching qualified for graduation, and who had passed, in any three or more science or arts subjects, special examinations up to the standard of the M.A. degree. The lectures, which were of the same nature as those given by the professors within the walls of the University, were largely attended, the numbers varying in the different classes from a minimum of four to a maximum of 265, and were continued until, on the removal of the legal disability which had previously stood in the way, the University itself was thrown open.

At Glasgow the initiative was taken by certain professors, who began in 1868 to give courses of lectures, some held in the University and some elsewhere, each professor making his own arrangements. In 1877 an Association for the higher education of women was formed, and courses of lectures were organised, which were given in the University by permission of the Senate. In 1877 also the Local Examinations, which from the outset were for both boys and girls, were started, and later, a Higher Certificate for women was instituted. In 1883 the Association for the higher education of women was incorporated under the name of Queen Margaret College, the Senate of the University appointing two members of its Executive Council, and lectures were given in the College buildings.

At St. Andrews, an Association for the promotion of the higher education of women was formed in 1868, and courses of lectures were given to women by University professors, which however were ultimately discontinued. In 1876 the University instituted an examination and diploma for women, with the title of L.L.A.

At Aberdeen, the Local Examinations instituted in 1880 were from the first open to girls. No other step was taken by the University as a body for the education of women, until the legal disability, which had impeded the action of all the Scotch Universities, was removed.

In 1889 an Act, entitled the Universities (Scotland) Act, gave power to Commissioners under the said Act to enable each University to admit women to graduation in one or more faculties, and to provide for their instruction; and in course of time the Commissioners issued an Ordinance, which on June 28th, 1892 became law, containing the following Regulations:

"I. It shall be in the power of the University Court of each University to admit women to graduation in such Faculty or Faculties as the said Court may think fit.

"II. It shall be competent to the University Court, after consultation with the Senatus, to make provision within the University for the instruction of women in any of the subjects taught within the University, either by admitting them to the ordinary classes, or by instituting separate classes for their instruction. Such classes shall be conducted by the professors or lecturers in the several subjects, or by lecturers specially appointed for the purpose by the University Court, provided always that the Court shall not institute classes where men and women shall be taught together, except after consultation with the Senatus. . . .

"IV. So soon as within any of the said Faculties in any University provision is made for the instruction of women in all subjects qualifying for graduation in which provision is made for the instruction of men, the conditions for the graduation of women within such Faculty shall be the same as the conditions for the graduation of men.

"VI. Women who may attend classes in any University must matriculate in that University, paying a fee of the same amount as that exigible for other students. . . .

"VII. It shall be the duty of any University Court which may exercise the power conferred by this Ordinance to make regulations for the use by women of such libraries and museums as are open to matriculated students of the University."*

The Ordinance was enabling, not compulsory, but each of the Universities concerned availed itself of its new powers without delay. Edinburgh, St. Andrews, and Aberdeen have opened their Science and Arts Classes to women. At Glasgow, Queen Margaret College has been transferred to the University, which appoints professors and lecturers. Some of the classes are mixed and are held in the University; the remainder are held separately in Queen Margaret College. In the four Universities a considerable number of women are preparing for graduation, and on some degrees have already been conferred.

While these important steps were being taken in the North, the Association for promoting the education of women in Oxford was also moving. In 1894 the Council asked the Local Examinations Delegacy to provide that women who had followed the B.A. course should receive a diploma, while an alternative course should entitle to a certificate. The Delegates

* Sections III. and V. and parts of II. and VI. are of a temporary nature. Ordinances as to Bursaries, etc., which also come within the scope of the Commission, have been subsequently issued.

suggested a modification of the proposal, removing from it all recognition of residence, and the Council thereupon withdrew their petition. After much further discussion, it was resolved at a meeting of the Association held on May 4th, 1895, "That it is desirable that women students who have complied with the statutable conditions as regards residence and examinations, should be admitted to the B.A. degree; and that a University diploma, recording their residence and qualification, should be granted to women students who have resided at least three years, have passed a preliminary and an intermediate examination, and have obtained a class in any Honour examination recognised in the University"; and further, "That this meeting approves of application being now made to the University for the admission of duly qualified women to the B.A. degree."

A petition to the Hebdomadal Council was accordingly circulated for signature among members of Convocation, those who were willing to sign being asked to indicate whether they preferred the alternative of admission to the B.A. degree, or that of the grant of a University diploma. The memorials, and two others to a contrary effect, having been presented, the Hebdomadal Council appointed a Committee to report upon them, and after receiving their report, submitted certain resolutions to Congregation. The first of these was as follows:

"That it is desirable, subject to certain conditions, to admit to the degree of B.A. women who have kept residence at Oxford for twelve terms in a place of residence approved by the Univer-

sity, and who have passed (under the same regulations as apply to undergraduates) all the examinations required for the degree of B.A."

This having been rejected on March 3rd, 1896, the other resolutions in which substitutes for the degree were proposed, were voted upon on March 10th, and also rejected. The women students are therefore in the same position in relation to the University as before the effort was made. On the other hand, it has been ascertained that a large amount of valuable support, which had before been latent, can now be relied upon. The controversy has brought out testimony, weighty both in itself and as coming from those whose experience and judgment lend authority to their words, in favour of the policy of the Association for promoting the education of women in Oxford. Its advocates are not discouraged, and there is no doubt that the question will again be raised on the first fitting opportunity.

The proceedings at Oxford and elsewhere have naturally been watched with interest at Cambridge, and could scarcely fail to awaken sympathy and stir to action. In the autumn of 1895, the Associates of Newnham College having brought the matter before the Council of the College, a Committee was appointed to confer with resident members of the University and with representatives of Girton College. As a result of mutual consultation, two Committees were formed, one of resident members of the Senate, the other of supporters of Girton and Newnham Colleges, and arrangements were made for memorialising the Council of the Senate in favour of the admission of women to degrees in the University. Four memorials were presented, one of which, signed by 2088 members of the Senate, stated that in their opinion the time had arrived for re-opening the question, and asked for the nomination of a Syndicate "to consider on what conditions and with what restrictions, if any, women should be admitted to degrees in the University." This was supported by a general memorial, to which 268 signatures were attached, and by two others, signed respectively by 164 Headmistresses of Endowed and Proprietary Schools, and by 1172 students of Girton and Newnham Colleges. In response to this appeal, the Council recommended and the Senate passed on March 12th, 1896, the following Grace:

"That a Syndicate be appointed to consider what further rights or privileges, if any, should be granted to women students by the University, and whether women should be made admissible to degrees in the University, and if so to what degrees, on what conditions, and with what restrictions, if any; that the Syndicate have power to consult with such bodies and persons as they may think fit; and that they report to the Senate before the end of the Michaelmas Term 1896."

Following upon this action of the Senate, memorials were circulated by a Committee of residents opposed to the granting of the degree.

Having now submitted a statement, which though by no means complete, may be accepted as presenting the principal stages of the movement now occupying the attention of the University of Cambridge, I venture to proceed to a brief examination, in the light of experience, of the proposed new departure.*

It may be gathered from the recent controversy that there are two parties concerned, the women students and the University—in regard to both of which the same questions may be put, *i.e.* what, if anything, would be gained—or lost—by the concession of membership of the University to duly qualified women? What it is believed that women would gain has been set forth in memorials and otherwise. For information as to what would be lost, we have to look to opponents. Their views have been stated in the discussion in the Arts School on Feb. 26th, in the above mentioned memorials, and in circulars issued by their promoters, as well as in sundry fly-sheets which have been circulated in the University. From these statements it appears that the drawbacks which it is feared, in the interests of women, would attach to the granting of the Degree are mainly, that it might act injuriously on the education of women from childhood upwards, by fettering it and causing it to be unduly assimilated to that of men; that it would intensify competition with men, which is in itself held to be undesirable; and that the cost of the education of women students would be increased by the payment of the University dues.

---

* See Appendix A. for Chronological Table (p.197). I have refrained from pursuing the course which has resulted in opening the profession of Medicine to women, although the first steps towards obtaining degrees were taken by women desirous of entering that profession, on the ground that the field is so large and so much has been done in it, that it could not conveniently be treated as a branch of the general movement.

As to the first of these objections, it may be observed that those who have asked for the degrees have throughout been in very large proportion men and women directly or indirectly concerned in the education of girls;* not High School mistresses only, but such bodies as the National Union for improving the education of women of all classes, the London and Birmingham Ladies' Educational Associations, the Rugby Council for promoting the education of women, the London Association of Schoolmistresses (largely composed of teachers of private schools), and the Governors of schools in various parts of the country; and that the question has been definitely before them during more than thirty years, having been publicly raised in the University of London as long ago as 1862, and no less than thirteen memorials asking for the Cambridge Degree having been presented in 1880. Is it likely that all these competent authorities would thoughtlessly combine in asking for a measure calculated to injure the cause they were anxious to promote? And can it be necessary after forty-eight years of experiments and progress to wait for twenty-five years more, as has been suggested, in order that posterity may obtain at that distant date, "a well considered expression of opinion from highly educated women as to what is on the whole the best education for the average members of their sex"?

As regards the assimilation of the education of

---

* See Appendix B. (p. 200).

women to that of men, it should be remembered that women have been invited to take up courses of study originally devised for men only, by the opening to them of the Previous Examination and the Triposes, and have pursued them with marked success. It may be observed also, that while there has always been a considerable substratum of similarity in the education of the sexes, the increasing approximation, which of late years has been going on in the higher grades, has been by no means all on one side. During this period Cambridge has added to its Triposes, Natural Sciences, History, and Mediaeval and Modern Languages; the examinations in Music have been put on a more satisfactory footing, and the changes in the Classical Tripos, giving a more prominent place to Archaeology, have encouraged the study of ancient Art. The subjects of the Final Special Examinations for the Ordinary Degree include History, Botany, Music, English, French, and German, all usually regarded as feminine studies. It may be mentioned also as a curious incident, that the Women's Examination instituted in 1869, designed to meet the needs of women, was four years later thrown open to men, under the name of the Higher Local Examinations.

As to the liberty accorded to women students at Cambridge, which they are exhorted not to throw away,—what is it? Simply the option of an alternative for the Previous Examination, which may be easier or harder according to the bent of the student and her previous preparation. It lightens the requirements in language, exacting no more than a pass in the Higher Local in one foreign language, which need not be Latin or Greek; but on the other hand, the demands in mathematics are more severe, and to some students Greek is easier than mathematics. Be that as it may, women have shown how little they value the alternative by passing it by. At the beginning, only about half of the Tripos candidates took it, and the number has been steadily diminishing, until now about three-fourths prefer the regular undergraduate course.

The evil of over-zealous competition is one which it is clearly desirable to check in both men and women, but the observation, that by the admission of women to university membership "it is obvious that the competition with men . . . . . would be intensified," must surely have been made by inadvertence. There is competition for places in the Class Lists, in which the names of women appear under the present system, but hardly for the degree, as to which a Senior Wrangler has no advantage over the man who stands last on the Poll.

The objection raised in the interest of women, that access to the degree would increase the cost of their education, will probably not be pressed. It is not proposed to compel any woman to be a B.A. against her will. If she considers the degree worth what it costs, that is her own concern. We do not hear that in the Universities in which a large number of women have graduated, the requirement that they should pay fees "of the same amount as that exigible for other students "—to use the Scotch phrase— has proved a difficulty.

There remains to be considered the loss, or the gain, to the University. Those who are opposed to the change believe that it would entail consequences injurious to the University as a place of education for men. The grounds for this belief appear to be, that as it would be unfair to maintain the rule restricting women to Tripos examinations, there would probably be a considerable number of women preparing for Pass examinations; that a great increase of numbers would necessitate either the creation of fresh hostels, or the admission of non-collegiate students, and that the problem of maintaining discipline thus imposed on the University would be extremely difficult; that in case this great increase should take place, it is not improbable that the University would be pressed to remodel its system of examinations, mainly in the interests of women; and further, that admission to the B.A. would speedily be followed by an agitation, which it would then be much harder to resist, for admission to the M.A. and a full share in the government of the University. Apprehensions have also been expressed as to the overcrowding of examinations and of lecture rooms, and attention has been called to the grievance that men's colleges are taxed for maintaining an education in which women have a share.

It may be observed that these forebodings are mainly based on the assumption that the concession of the desired privilege would largely increase the number of women students. It is thus tacitly admitted that the privilege would be highly appreciated by young women all over the country, and also that they would have the sympathy of their parents and guardians, as women of the undergraduate age rarely have money at their command, and could not make use of the opportunity offered without the sanction of their friends, who would no doubt be influenced in giving or refusing their sanction by the prevailing opinion of their class.

The fear that if the Ordinary Degree were accessible, Cambridge would be overrun by a crowd of Poll-women, is surely fanciful. To the pleasure-seeking young lady, the chance of being a B.A. after three years of distasteful occupation under considerable restraint, could hardly be a powerful attraction; and if it were, the colleges could take care of themselves. A strong college can protect itself; to a weak college, or one mainly bent on filling its rooms with wealthy idlers, the present University regulations for female students would be a very inadequate safeguard. They deprive the college authorities of the use of their discretion in choosing what they may have reason to believe to be the best course for some of their students, but they do not preclude the admission of nominal students making no pretence of preparing for any examination. The mere withholding of the Ordinary Degree cannot be regarded as in itself a security against the intrusion of the frivolous persons whom it is desirable to keep at a distance.

Women in the Universities

As to the probability of a great accession of students, there is a strong opinion that it would be kept in check by want of means on the part of those who would most value a University course. Judging by experience, it seems likely that there would be an increase, but that it would come slowly, not by leaps and bounds, and there would thus be ample time for such developments as might be required to meet it. It is obvious that women could not come up and matriculate unless accommodation had been first provided for them, and the recognition of fresh hostels would be within the discretion of the University. As to the necessity of admitting women as non-collegiate students, the system was only adopted for men in 1869, and the University could be under no obligation to extend it to women.

The difficulty as to discipline is perhaps more strongly felt than is shown in published statements, but it does not appear to be insuperable. There is no reason to suppose that either Girton or Newnham would object to their students being subjected to proctorial supervision, but experience gives good ground for believing that it would be superfluous. The wisest course would appear to be that which is already practically in force, *i.e.*, that of leaving to the college authorities, who are *in loco parentis*, the responsibility of maintaining good order, with, however, the additional precaution of requiring that any college recognised by the University should hold a license as a public hostel, which could be revoked on occasion. There is the more reason to hope that such a provision for the maintenance of order would be effectual, as there are at present a considerable number of young women, of the same age and class as the college students, who, while residing at Cambridge are not under proctorial jurisdiction, home guidance and their own good sense and good feeling being sufficient safeguards.

The apprehension that in some remote future the system of University examinations might be remodelled mainly in the interests of women, may be met by the consideration that the tendency of late years has been to make changes, in the interests of men, in the direction of assimilation to the education of women; while on the other hand, some changes have been made, in the interests of women, in the assimilation to that of men. Perhaps the explanation may be that, when both parties are seeking the best, what is best for the human being is found to be also the best for both sexes.

With regard to the fear that the granting of the B.A. would be speedily followed by an agitation for the M.A. and a share in the government of the University, it would be rash to prophesy, but looking back upon the past, it may perhaps be safely predicted that whatever may be done in the future will not be done incautiously or in haste. The memorialists for degrees have asked for consideration as to what restrictions, if any, should accompany the granting of the degree, and have thus shown themselves ready to accept such limitations of privilege as may be deemed expedient, and there could be no difficulty in inserting in the statute empowering admission to degrees, such restrictive provisions as after due deliberation might be held to be desirable.

A few words may be added as to matters of detail. The possible crowding of examination and lecture-rooms does not appear to be a formidable difficulty. It is calculated that the admission of women to membership would add to the income of the University at least £1500 a year, that being the difference between the amount which would be paid by Girton and Newnham students in University dues and that now paid by them for examinations only. It is clear that this sum yearly would much more than cover any expenses which would be incurred for enlargement of buildings, and even, if it should in some cases be found desirable, the duplication of lectures. It is not alleged that as yet there has been any serious overcrowding, so that the alterations required cannot be on a large scale. If the accession of numbers, which is anticipated by some, should take place, there would be a corresponding increase of revenue. That the University should have this large sum placed at its disposal, enabling it to meet demands for improved appliances which are now reluctantly put aside on account of their costliness, may fairly be reckoned as a not inconsiderable gain; while, looking at the University as " an incorporation of students in all and every of the liberal arts and sciences "—whose colleges were founded "for the study of learning and knowledge, and for the better service of Church and State "—may it not be reasonably urged that these high objects could hardly be better promoted than by so widening its range of membership as to secure a larger number of zealous and capable students? For it should be remembered, that the instruction and discipline which the students receive are not a benefit to themselves only. What they have gained they transmit to others, and through them the University may wield an increasing influence on the education of girls, and indirectly on that of the nation at large. In the memorial lately presented to the Council by Headmistresses, it is pointed out that "the whole character of school studies has been raised and strengthened by the influence of University standards"; that "the women's colleges have supplied the schools with more highly educated teachers than could otherwise have been obtained, and to this cause must be ascribed much of the remarkable progress made during recent years in the education of girls." The memorialists are "anxious that this influence of the University on the schools should be extended and confirmed." It is true that this extension of influence would entail extended responsibility, but there is responsibility incurred by refusing opportunities of usefulness as well as by accepting them, and Englishmen are not wont to hold back when called upon to occupy ever widening spheres of beneficent activity. Cambridge has already done much for women, and it can hardly be denied that the honour of the University, justly dear to its sons, has thereby been enhanced. May we not hope that the boon which is now sought may be one of those gifts which are twice blessed—blessing both him that gives and him that takes.

April 30th, 1896.

APPENDIX.

A. (*See p.* 187)

CHRONOLOGICAL TABLE.

1848 and 1849.
Foundation of Queen's College and Bedford College, London.

1856.
Application for admission to University of London; rejected on legal opinion.

1862.
Proposal to obtain modification of Charter of University of London; rejected by casting vote of Chancellor.

Formation of Committee for obtaining the admission of women to university examinations.

1863.
Informal examination of girls by Cambridge Local Examiners.

1865 and 1866.
Cambridge, Edinburgh, and Durham Local Examinations opened to girls.

1868.
Examinations for women instituted by University of London.

1869.
College for women opened at Hitchin.

Formation of Edinburgh Association for university education of women.

Women's examinations instituted at Cambridge.

Questions relating to Women

1870.

Oxford Local Examinations opened to girls.

Informal examination of women students for Cambridge Previous Examination.

1871.

House of residence opened for women attending lectures at Cambridge.

1872.

Incorporation of College for women under the name of Girton College.

Informal examination of women students for Cambridge Mathematical and Classical Triposes.

1873.

Removal of Girton College to Cambridge.

Oxford and Cambridge Schools Examinations instituted for boys and girls.

1874.

Certificate for women instituted by University of Edinburgh.

Memorials to University of London for admission to Degrees.

1875.

Newnham Hall opened at Cambridge.

1876.

Diploma for women with title of of L.L.A., instituted at St. Andrews.

1877.

Women's Examinations instituted at Oxford.

Formation of Glasgow Association for higher education of women.

Glasgow Local Examinations for boys and girls instituted.

1878.

Admission to membership and degrees of University of London.

Women in the Universities

1879.

Lady Margaret Hall and Somerville Hall opened at Oxford.

1880.

Foundation of Victoria University for men and women.

Memorials for admission to Cambridge degrees, and appointment of Syndicate thereon.

Aberdeen Local Examinations for boys and girls instituted.

1881 and 1882.

Admission to Cambridge Degree Examinations in Honours; and in Music.

1883.

Association for higher education of women in Glasgow incorporated under the name of Queen Margaret College.

1884 and 1886.

Admission to Oxford Honour Moderations and Final Honour Schools of Mathematics, Natural Science, and Modern History; and to Responsions.

1887.

Memorials for admission to Cambridge degrees.

1888 and 1890.

Admission to Oxford Final Honour Schools of Literae Humaniores, and of Jurisprudence, and to Final Examination for B.Mus.

1892.

Admission to Membership and Degrees of Universities of Edinburgh, Glasgow, St. Andrews, and Aberdeen.

1893 and 1894.

Admission to Oxford Honour Schools of Theology and Oriental Studies; to Examination for D.Mus.; and to all B.A. Degree Examinations not previously open.

1895.

Admission to Degrees, in all faculties except of Theology, of University of Durham.

Memorial to Oxford Hebdomadal Council for admission to B.A. Degree.

Questions relating to Women

Alternative Resolutions in favour of admission to B.A. Degree, or some substitute for it, submitted by Oxford Hebdomadal Council to Congregation, and rejected.

Memorials to Council of Senate of the University of Cambridge for nomination of Syndicate to consider question of admission to Degrees. Grace for appointment of Syndicate assed by Senate.

B. (*See p.* 188)

Memorials asking for the admission of women to Degrees have been presented to the Universities of London and Cambridge respectively, in 1874, in 1880, and in 1887, by the following bodies interested in female education:—

Committee of the Birmingham Ladies' Educational Association.

Committee of the Queen's Institute of female Professional Schools, Dublin.

Central Committee of National Association for improving the education of women.

Leeds Association of Schoolmistresses.

Rugby Council for promoting the education of women.

Executive Committee of Ladies' Educational Association, London.

Managers of University College, Nottingham.

London Association of Schoolmistresses.

Governors of Bradford Girls' Grammar School.

Council of St. Andrews School for Girls.

Council of Teachers' Training and Registration Society.

Governors of Salt Schools, Shipley.

Trustees of Manchester High School for Girls.

Council of Edgbaston High School for Girls.

Local Secretaries for Local Examinations and Lectures.

Headmistresses of Endowed and Proprietary Schools.

Assistant-Mistresses in Endowed and Proprietary Schools.

The Women's Suffrage Movement.

[*The Girton Review for the Lent and Easter Terms*, 1905.]

I

WHY SHOULD WE CARE FOR IT?

IN conversing with Old Students of Women's Colleges on the subject of Women's Suffrage, I have found—and I believe others have had the same experience—that comparatively few seriously object to it, but also that not many care much about it. The indifference may probably be traced, for the most part, to one general cause, that of pre-occupation with other interests. No one can care eagerly for an unlimited number of objects, and Old Students have much to think of. Those who are married and have young children, with perhaps rather small means, have domestic cares of an absorbing nature, while those who are unmarried are as a rule engaged in professional or unpaid work, as teachers, doctors, nurses, secretaries, Poor-Law Guardians, managers of schools, etc. They are anxious to do their best in their several callings, and to lose no opportunity of perfecting themselves for their work, to which they apply themselves with whole-hearted zeal. Must we not admire and sympathise with this eager devotion to the duty that lies nearest? Yet, must we not recognise that there are other duties which should not be disregarded?

The indifference to the Women's Suffrage movement, though it may be explained, is not therefore justified, and I want to ask those who say, " Oh, yes,

I am in favour of it, of course, but I don't do any-thing," or, " I don't know much about it," or, " I don't see any particular use in it," to consider some reasons for caring about it, and doing what they can to help it forward.

Perhaps it may be best to begin by a plain state-ment of the object of the Women's Suffrage Societies, *i.e.*, to obtain the extension of the Parliamentary franchise to women on the same terms as it is, or may be, granted to men.

It will be seen that the object does not include seats in Parliament. Some people, if you speak of the Parliamentary vote, at once reply, " I do not want to have women in Parliament "—which is some-what irrelevant. As to what may happen a hundred years hence, when social conditions may be widely different to what they are now, we do not undertake to predict. For the present, the question of women in Parliament is not practical politics.

Nor would the removal of the special disability imposed upon women make all grown-up women voters. It is estimated that the effect of the measure proposed would be to add to the six millions of male voters about one million women. The disproportion arises from the action of Household Suffrage, which gives one vote to each household. When the house-holder is a widow or unmarried woman, the vote would fall to her, but in the great majority of cases, the householder being a man, he would have the vote. Married women, having landed property in their own right, would be entitled to the vote; but these would, of course, be a minute proportion of the whole electorate.

Again, it is not proposed to make the vote compulsory. I have heard an Old Girtonian say that she had enough responsibilities already, and did not wish for any addition to them. If she should wish to avoid the responsibility of choosing between rival candidates, her course would be easy. She need not vote for either. I should like to remind her, however, that if she makes known that she does not want the vote, she cannot escape the responsibility of helping to hinder its being granted to other women who do want it.

I have been dealing in negations, and I have another negative statement to make. I do not agree with those advocates of Women's Suffrage—and they are many—who urge that if women have the vote, this or that reform, which they themselves desire, would be carried. The small proportion of women who would be added to the electorate could scarcely exercise any very powerful direct influence on legislation, even if they were unanimous, and whatever else may be doubtful, it is certain that women will not be all of one mind, even on subjects that may be regarded as specially concerning them. Speaking for myself only, I do not believe that many rapid and direct changes in our laws would follow upon the extension of the suffrage to women.

Then, it may be said, if you do not expect that women will do any good by their use of voting power, why do you wish for it?

Questions relating to Women

My reply is that though I do not expect that any great effect of the women's vote would at once be seen in the shape of extensive legislative reform, I do expect that, gradually, laws which are unjust to women—and without going into detail, one may note that there *are* such laws—would disappear, and that women would gain a hearing on questions in regard to which the conditions of their lives may give them special knowledge and insight. But I look at the whole question from a somewhat different point of view. I desire the removal of the disability which in my opinion is unjustly and unwisely inflicted upon women, because I believe that indirectly it would have a deep and far-reaching effect; that by raising the status of all women, as such, it would tend gradually to remove hindrances to their well-being, to increase their self-respect and their sense of responsibility, and to favour their development on true and natural lines. Would it improve their economic position? In plain words, would it raise the wages of inadequately paid women workers? This is a serious and a difficult question. It is some-times argued that as the wages of working-men have risen since they obtained the Parliamentary vote, the same result would follow in the case of women. I am not myself convinced by this argument, as it must be remembered that it is since the extension of the franchise to working-men that they have obtained the right of combination, and as this has already been secured for women as well as men, it is difficult to see what more could be done to help them by legislation. But here, as elsewhere, one may look with confidence for happy results from a general rise in the status of women, which may be hoped for as a consequence of their recognition by the State as responsible citizens. This view seems to be taken by the well-known Labour leader, Mr. Keir Hardie. In a speech addressed to women textile workers in 1902, he said, " By treating women—I am speaking now from a working-class point of view—as equals, by conceding to them every concession which men claim for themselves, the women will play the part of the equal, not only in regard to wages, but in all other matters appertaining to industrial life. . . . The possession of the Franchise itself would give women a new standing, a new increase of power, and would enable them to win for themselves concessions which are to-day withheld."

Taking the case of what is called the educated class, we might fairly hope that if women were recognised as equal before the law, the inequitable distribution of educational endowments might be rectified, and barriers placed in the way of securing professional instruction and status might be removed. As to the former, I may mention such examples as that of the Hitchin Grammar School scheme, which lays down that the Head Master is to have a fixed salary (apart from capitation fees) of £150, and the Head Mistress, with similar duties and qualifications, £100; and the " Scheme for the management of Harpur's Charity at Bedford," which enacts that the Governors shall apportion funds " applicable to the Grammar School

and High School between such Schools, in proportion
to the average number of scholars attending the same
respectively during the preceding year, but reckoning,
for this purpose, three boys as earning the same
amount as five girls."

As an example of closing the door of a profession
undeniably suitable for women, I may cite a case
which may come home specially to the readers of the
Girton Review. Some years ago, an Old Girtonian
desired to become an accountant by profession, and
a member of the Institute of Chartered Accountants.
She was prepared to fulfil all the prescribed conditions. One, which might have been an insuperable
difficulty, was happily met by the discovery of a
Chartered Accountant who was willing to take her
as an articled clerk. The Committee of the Society
for Promoting the Employment of Women sent in a
memorial to the Council of the Institute asking
permission for women to present themselves for the
examinations in due course, with a view to ultimate
admission to membership. The permission was
refused, and though women are practising as public
accountants, they do so more or less as amateurs,
having no legal qualification. Such cases might be
dealt with by law, as the educational endowments
are public property, and the privilege of holding a
Royal Charter of Incorporation might presumably
be made conditional upon opening the door to all
properly qualified applicants for admission; but I
should hope for the dying out of such injustices
through the infusion of a new spirit of equity in

our national life, without recourse to legal enact-
ments.

Let us now come to a matter which lies very near
home, the question of membership of the Universities
of Oxford and Cambridge. It has been, I think,
tacitly agreed, since the great defeat at Cambridge
in 1897, that, for the present, it would be useless
to make any fresh appeal to the Universities. But
if such a step were taken as the granting of the
Parliamentary Suffrage to women, the situation
would be materially altered. It was found, I think,
during the agitation for degrees, that the objection
most strongly felt by our opponents was that the
admission to degrees would carry with it partici-
pation in the government of the University. When
our petition was modestly limited to the B.A., it was
pointed out that the B.A.'s. would want to proceed to
M.A., as no doubt they would—and they would then
become members of the Senate, entitled to vote and
to hold office. But if women were taking part in
the government of the whole country, a share in the
government of the University might surely be granted
as a natural consequence, and the long-fought battle
might come to a peaceful close.

II

How can we help to further it?

If any Old Student has become convinced that,
however apart from ordinary philanthropy, and however wanting in such immediately visible results

Questions relating to Women

as may be hoped for in other fields of work, the Women's Suffrage movement may claim at least some share of effort, the question follows—" What can I do to help it forward ? "

The ways of helping are many and various. I will mention first, the most simple and obvious, that of joining one of the Societies, of which there are about thirty in different parts of the country, including the Central, to which I myself belong. This Society, besides being metropolitan, has as its area of work all parts of England which are not covered by any other Society. With such a field of work, it has, as may be supposed, enough, and more than enough, to do. Anyone can become a member by signing a form expressing approval of the object, and contributing annually any sum from a shilling upwards. As a matter of fact the subscriptions range in amount from one shilling to five guineas. For my own part, I am disposed to value personal service so much more than money, that it costs me something of an effort even to suggest anything which involves the payment of a subscription, but some people who would gladly give work and are unavoidably prevented from doing so, can give money —and it would be foolish to forget that war cannot be carried on without sinews. As every year old members are removed by death and other causes, their places want filling up, and with the greater development of the work fresh needs arise. Our offices, which also provide accommodation for the Executive Committee of the National Union of

Women's Suffrage Societies, consist of two small rooms, and are inconveniently and at times, I am afraid, unhealthily crowded. We certainly want more space, and in the present condition of our Treasury it is questionable whether removal to larger offices would be prudent. A similar difficulty stands in the way of adding to the staff, which might be done with advantage to the work, if funds permitted.

A mode of helping, which is both easy and useful, is to circulate instructive literature, lending or giving leaflets and tracts suited to the particular case, to friends who have not yet seriously considered the subject. And when appealing to the most highly educated body of women in the kingdom, may we not ask them to turn their gifts to account in producing literature, both substantial and attractive? Articles in magazines and newspapers may reach readers not before approached, and paragraphs in local papers on any and every occasion which may furnish a good excuse for bringing the question forward, may be very useful. Persons experienced in such matters say that the best plan is, not to offer material to an Editor, asking him to make use of it, but to supply the article or the paragraph cut and dried. By thus taking trouble, instead of giving it, we work upon the lines of least resistance.

Good service may also be done by getting into communication with Societies in which discussion is carried on, as, *e.g.*, Political Associations, such as Habitations of the Primrose League and Women's Liberal Associations, Local Parliaments, Clubs, etc.

Questions relating to Women

[1905

The subject is often not unwelcome, but suitable speakers are wanted, and Old Students who in their College Debating Societies have learnt to speak clearly and to the point might take a useful part in discussions. As elements of suitability, knowledge of the subject, and a genial, persuasive attitude are needed. I mention this, because I hear so much of the harm that is done by aggressive, intolerant advocacy. It may be said, of course, that a cause ought not to be judged by the manners and appearance of its advocates, and that in a large movement for reform it cannot be expected that all its adherents will be unfailing in good sense, good feeling, and good taste; but we must make allowance for human nature, and there can be no doubt that the success of our cause depends to some extent on the demeanour of its supporters. Gentleness, moderation in argument, and readiness to hear the other side, may disarm opposition, even if they do not always convince.

A new departure has lately been made in the way of meetings, at which Old Students, whether practised speakers or not, might give welcome help. We owe the idea, which is a modification of the old plan of drawing-room meetings, to our Treasurer, Mrs. Sterling. The new plan is to avoid formality, or anything like an imitation, on a small scale, of a public meeting. It is an afternoon party, at which, instead of music, or a conjuror, or talk about the weather, Women's Suffrage is the entertainment. The hostess invites her friends and acquaintances, often without knowing whether they are for or against it, or simply very much in the dark about it. She makes use of her own visiting cards, writing on the back:

AT HOME

---

to meet_____for talk on Women's Suffrage.
Tea at 4 p.m.

Tea is served before, not after, the meeting, and while partaking of the cup which cheers but not inebriates, the guests fall into a social mood, and are prepared for the friendly interchange of views which is to follow. The specially invited guest then says a few words by way of opening, and conversation in a somewhat exact sense, *i.e.*, not a Babel of talk all over the room, follows. It is the special feature of these meetings that, being genuinely informal, people are not afraid to speak, as they usually are at the old-fashioned drawing-room meetings, however pressingly invited. It is a mode of "peaceful penetration" into dark places, often leading to annexation. Sometimes friends are brought to light and made useful, and there are many conversions. The meetings—or afternoon parties as they should perhaps be called—are much enjoyed. It constantly happens that one or more of the ladies present undertakes to have a similar gathering at her own house, and thus the light is spread into new quarters.

A good deal has been done, and much remains to be done, in the way of organising work in the constituencies. This may be done by forming either local committees, or branches, which may grow into independent societies, in connection with some existing society. In the metropolitan district, and perhaps in small places generally, a local committee may be found to work well. In large towns it may be advisable to adopt the more ambitious form of organisation. I happen to have access to information in regard to what may be taken as samples of each sort, *i.e.*, the Marylebone Local Committee and the Croydon Branch, both connected with the Central Society, and a sketch of the rise and progress in each case may be helpful.

On April 19th, 1904, five ladies, of whom I was one, met and formed themselves into a Committee (with power to add to their number) for work in Marylebone in connection with the Central Society for Women's Suffrage. We decided to make it our first business to get together an influential list of supporters, and in order that there might be no risk of mistake as to what our friends were committing themselves to, they were asked to sign the following form:—

MADAM,—You have my permission to include my name in a list of residents or owners of property in the Borough of East or West Marylebone who are in favour of the extension of the Parliamentary franchise to women on the same terms as it is, or may be, granted to men.

*Name*_____

Address _____

*Date*_____

We also had a form printed, with a suitable heading, for a list of names, which, as soon as they became sufficiently numerous, were also printed, *pour encourager les autres*. We made it our aim to obtain the names of ladies and gentlemen respected by their neighbours, and not chiefly known as pronounced advocates of Women's Rights. In order to intensify the list, we asked, as a rule, for only one name from each household, and when it was a case of husband and wife both in favour we preferred the husband on the ground that being already a voter his name would be more influential with Parliamentary candidates and their leading supporters, whom we specially wished to impress. We were encouraged by meeting with sympathy in quarters in which it had not before been manifested. In a few months we made such progress as seemed to justify our announcing ourselves to the Marylebone public, and a paragraph appeared in a leading local paper, headed,

"THE WOMEN'S SUFFRAGE MOVEMENT
STRONG SUPPORT FROM MARYLEBONE"

and giving a selection from the names on our list, consisting chiefly of professional men and women, leading tradesmen, and ladies in an independent position. We are still enlisting adherents, and lately there has been a further announcement of influential names. It has been arranged that the expenses of printing, etc., are met by the Central Society, on the understanding that the subscriptions of Marylebone supporters are paid to the parent Society. I may add that the amount of the local contribution to the funds of the Society has been considerably in excess of the local outlay, which has been very small.

The Borough of Croydon, containing about 140,000 inhabitants, furnishes an excellent example of organisation on a larger scale. Here, chiefly through the instrumentality of an Old Student of Newnham, Mrs. St. George Reid (*née* Martyn), a branch Society has been started. The Borough is divided into six wards, and in each ward a small committee has been formed, with its own secretary, who keeps a register of members within her ward, collects their subscriptions, and arranges drawing-room or garden meetings. The ward secretaries have proved a great success. They come into contact with a much larger circle than could be reached by one secretary, and there is a healthy rivalry between the wards, stimulating the increase of membership and activity in holding meetings. The general control of the branch is in the hands of a committee, at present provisional; when the branch is more fully organised, the Provisional Committee is to be superseded by an Executive Committee, representative of the six wards into which the Borough is divided. Such a thorough piece of work must strike some of us as more easy to admire than to imitate, but we may look upon it as an ideal to work up to, so far as our circumstances and our capacities permit.

Looking at the conditions of the moment, with a General Election, not looming in the distance but near at hand, it seems obvious that attention should be specially directed to enlightening and persuading candidates for Parliament, and the energetic supporters who are likely to have a considerable share in directing their policy. At a meeting held in London last autumn, one of the speakers, Mr. Yoxall, M.P., gave some information and advice as to the Parliamentary position of Women's Suffrage. "From the House of Commons, from the inside point of view," said Mr. Yoxall, "it is an unpractical thing, and I think you will have to decide, as other bodies of people in this country have had to decide, to make your support of a political party contingent upon that party adopting the principles you support." Here an important question—what is called the test question—is raised, and before the Election comes it must be answered. It is said that on some occasion a lady was urging a labouring man to give his vote to the candidate of whom she approved. She was asked how she meant to give her own vote, and having replied that she had none, was met by the retort: "If you are not fit to vote yourself, how can you be fit to advise me how to vote?" The story, whether authentic, or only *ben trovato*, is surely much to the purpose. A firm refusal by women to canvass for a candidate who will not support their claim to the vote might bring home to the party politicians the absurdly anomalous position which women are urged to accept.

Mr. Yoxall went on to say: "Another obstacle in your way is that there is not a clear conception in the House of Commons as to what you exactly want.

Questions relating to Women

[1905

. . . Vague pledges have been given at General Elections, but the Women's Suffrage question is not a matter of daily and hourly conversation in the smoke-room. A Member of Parliament is not screwed up to the mark on this point by Resolutions, either from his constituents or his committees of workers, neither does he receive letters from constituents whom he strongly respects. . . What is your claim? I take it to be that whatever qualifies a man to vote for the election of Members to Parliament shall qualify a woman to vote also." That *is* our claim, briefly and comprehensively stated, and it seems to be necessary to lose no opportunity of making it plain—that this, and nothing else, is what we are asking for. Other cognate questions may claim consideration hereafter. When the time comes, let them be dealt with on their merits, in the light of experience, and with due consideration of such new conditions as may arise in the future. In the meantime, let us do all we can to fix attention on the immediately pressing question, and as regards candidates for Parliament, let us not be satisfied with the "vague pledges" to which Mr. Yoxall referred, or with anything less than an explicit statement in the Election address. Let us get Resolutions passed, letters written by electors who are strongly respected, committees of workers approached, and let no one be able to say, that women evidently do not want the vote, as they make no effort to get it.

All this means, it may be objected, that we are to make ourselves dreadful bores. I am afraid I must sorrowfully admit that this is at least partially true. To be a bore is one of the sacrifices that must be made, if we are to take part in carrying a great reform. We may become wearisome, even to ourselves, by incessant reiteration of what we have said so many times before. But there are bores and bores, and if we cannot help being tiresome, we may try to be as inoffensively tiresome as the necessities of the case admit.

It will be seen that there is much that needs to be done, much that can be done. The Old Students of the Women's Colleges, now numbered by thousands, can, if they will, in many ways give effectual service.

July, 1905.

Letters on Women's Suffrage

I

ARE WOMEN SUFFRAGISTS ASKING FOR SEATS IN PARLIAMENT? A REPLY

[*A Letter of inquiry, signed "Philogynist," appeared in "The Times" of January 30th, 1907. The following reply was inserted on February 4th.*]

SIR,—Your correspondent, "Philogynist," asks whether the advocates of Women's Suffrage "merely demand the right to vote at Parliamentary Elections, or do they desire that women should be given the chance of becoming Members of Parliament, as well as the power of voting," and complains, that to these questions, often asked, "never has an authoritative reply been vouchsafed."

Without making a too arrogant claim to speak with authority, may I, as the chosen representative of the Women's Suffrage Societies on the deputation to the Prime Minister last May, offer a few words in reply? To the first question, I answer, without hesitation, that the right to vote—and this only—is the demand of the Women's Suffrage Societies, formulated many years ago, and clearly stated in the authorised definition of their object, viz.: that it is "to obtain the Parliamentary Franchise for women on the same terms as it is, or may be, granted to men."

To the question, "How long it will be before the larger claim will be brought forward?" the only possible answer seems to be, Who can say? In a country where free speech is allowed, anybody may bring forward anything, but to the further question— "why it should not be made at once," I would ask attention to some considerations which may be held to constitute a reply.

To begin with, many of the advocates of Women's Suffrage are decidedly opposed to such a claim. Over and over again I have heard supporters of the movement declare that they do not wish to see women in Parliament, carefully guarding themselves from being suspected of any such desire.

Let me further point out that no one can be returned for Parliament except by some constituency, and that as after the proposed reform women would be in a minority of, say, one to five or six, a very large proportion of the male voters in a given constituency must desire to be represented by a woman in order to secure her election. Admitting, however, that in some exceptional constituencies such preference might conceivably be shown, the safeguard would still remain that the previously existing Parliament would consist entirely of men, and would be capable of passing an Act definitely excluding women. It may, no doubt, be said, that to give women seats in Parliament would be the logical consequence of giving them votes, but English Parliaments are not governed by logic, and that such action as I have indicated would not, though illogical, be unconstitutional, may be inferred from the fact that the clergy of the Church of England are ineligible for membership of Parliament, though they have the same right of voting as other citizens.

Surely it may be asserted with confidence that the question of women in Parliament is not practical politics, and we may urge upon our statesmen not to be scared by a bugbear, which, when fairly faced, loses all its terrors, but no longer to delay the carrying through of a just and moderate measure, which, while meeting the claim put forth by reasonable women, is also desirable in the larger interest of the whole community.

II

A CONSTITUTIONAL SLUICE, OR STEPS IN THE ENFRANCHISEMENT OF WOMEN

["THE Times" of November 29th, 1907, contained a leading article under the heading of "Adult Suffrage," commenting on a manifesto issued by the executive council of the Social Democratic party on the question of universal adult suffrage. In this manifesto it is said: "Socialists are warned not to be led away by the recent agitation among Englishwomen basing their demand for representation 'not on democratic and revolutionary principles, but on a worn-out middle-class theory of a property qualification.' This agitation, we are told, 'has disclosed the anomalous position of working women, agitating, suffering and going to prison for the sake of an electoral reform, which, if carried, would not only fail to enfranchise them politically, but would, through giving further representation to propertied interests, rivet still faster the chains of their political, economic, and social thraldom.'" "The Times" accepts these statements, "from the point of view of the Social Democratic party," but it warns "light-hearted supporters of Women Suffrage, on the basis of a property qualification," that "if they once succeed in obtaining Women Suffrage on this precarious and, in our judgment, illogical basis, then the property qualification becomes the only remaining constitutional barrier against what the Social Democratic party themselves call their 'revolutionary designs.' Once remove that barrier, and adult suffrage automatically comes to mean the enfranchisement of every adult woman in the United Kingdom. Is the dyke strong enough to withstand the pressure of the oncoming flood?" "The Times" is of opinion that "if, while the property qualification still exists, we close, bar, and bang the door against woman suffrage while we can, we at least avoid putting this tremendous weapon into the hands of a frankly revolutionary party. We may not succeed in damming back the democratic flood altogether . . . but at least we can keep the dykes up against it, and may perchance thereby regulate its revolutionary and destructive overflow—as has often been done in our constitutional history—by an ordered series of constitutional sluices."]

The following reply was inserted in "The Times" of December 25, 1907:—

SIR,— In the article on adult suffrage in your issue of November 29, the statement made by the executive committee of the Social Democratic party, that the present demand for women's suffrage is based on a "worn-out middle-class theory of a property qualification," seems to be accepted without question, and "the light-hearted supporters of women's suffrage on a property qualification" are advised to "consider very carefully the extreme seriousness of the prospect" opened up before us.

May I ask where these light-hearted persons are to be found? The object of the National Union of Women's Suffrage Societies is clearly stated to be "to obtain the Parliamentary suffrage for women on the same terms as it is, or may be, granted to men." These terms may be classified under six headings— i.e., property, occupation, residence, lodgers, freemen, the Universities. The position, that under these headings, women of property only would come in is obviously untenable, but the misrepresentation of the case has been persistently reiterated, and even the Prime Minister was so far misled as to state in the debate on March 8, on the Bill promoted by the Women's Suffrage Societies, that the Bill would enfranchise "a small minority of well-to-do single women"; and, again, "It will enfranchise the propertied and well-to-do ladies, but it will not touch, to any such degree as is necessary, the mass of working women of the country and the working men's wives." In reply, Mr. Philip Snowden, the distinguished Labour member, is reported to have "expressed his regret that the Prime Minister should lend the weight of his influence and authority to the statement that this Bill would not touch the working classes of the country, but would only add to the register a small minority of well-to-do women. . . . Some two or three years ago he supervised a census which was taken in about fifty different parts of the country, with the object of ascertaining what proportion of the women enfranchised by a measure of this sort would belong to the working classes. The definition of working women acted on was 'those who worked for wages, those domestically employed, and those who were supported by the earnings of wage-earning children.' The municipal registers examined contained 372,000 names, and the total number of women voters was 59,000, of whom about 82·4 per cent. were working women."

Lest from this statement another misconception should arise, and it should be assumed that what may be called manual workers would have an overwhelming preponderance among women voters, it should be remembered that the municipal and Parliamentary registers are not identical, and that women might be qualified for registration under one or other of the headings given above, although not on the municipal register. Wives would not necessarily be excluded. Married women holding landed property in their own right would be qualified, and a certain number would come in as graduates of the Universities. It may be mentioned also that the inhabitant occupier might be either husband or wife. No doubt in the great majority of cases the husband would be the occupier, but instances have come within my own personal knowledge in which, by mutual consent, the house has been taken in the name of the wife, who has thus been qualified for the municipal vote. The "limited Bill," as it is sometimes called, would enfranchise a comparatively small number of women—it is estimated at a million to a million and a half, as against some six or seven millions of male voters—but it is comprehensive, inasmuch as it would remove a stigma which the State, by denying the right to vote, inflicts on all women, as such, of whatever rank or condition.

The question of adult suffrage is entirely apart from that of women's suffrage, which means simply the removal, in regard to the Parliamentary vote, of a disability which has been already, to a great extent, abolished in other cases. In 1869 the Municipal Corporations Act restored to women ratepayers the vote in municipal elections, of which they had been deprived by the Municipal Corporation Act of 1835. In 1870 the Education Act, which created School Boards, placed women on the same footing as men, in regard both to the vote and eligibility to the Boards. In 1888 the County Electors Act gave women votes for the election of the county councils created by the Local Government Act of that year. In 1894 the Local Government Act confirmed the rights of women to all local franchises and their eligibility as Poor Law guardians and made them also eligible as parish and district councillors. In the present year, women have been made eligible to county and town councils. Corresponding advances have been made in domestic and social spheres. In the '70's the Married Women's Property Acts secured to married women rights of property previously denied. The Universities and the medical profession have been thrown open; women are serving the State as inspectors of factories, sanitary inspectors, &c., and, whereas, in earlier years, it was a new thing for women to give evidence before Royal Commissions, they now themselves occupy the seat of judgment as Commissioners. These successive steps may be taken as answering to the process described in your article as " an ordered series of constitutional sluices." Has not the time arrived for adding to the series another constitutional sluice, by the granting of Parliamentary franchise ? . . . .

III

CHRISTIAN TEACHING AND THE LESSONS OF EXPERIENCE ON IDEALS OF WOMANHOOD

[The following letter, addressed to the " Spectator " on the occasion of an article in the issue of July 25th, 1908, was not inserted.]

SIR,—In your article in this week's Spectator on the Women's National Anti-Suffrage League, you

Questions relating to Women

urge upon your readers never to forget that " women were born, not for struggle and battle, but rather for what is ' gentle, tranquil, true.' Man "—you say —" is a fighting animal and is often the better for a fight. . . . . With women it is just the reverse. Conflict, whether moral or physical, even when necessary, leaves traces on women that none can see without regret."

May I be allowed to point out what appears to me to be the inconsistency of this view with the teaching of Christ, especially as reflected in our English Liturgy, as well as with the facts of our daily life. In our Baptismal Service, which is the same for both sexes, the future woman is signed with the sign of the Cross, " in token that hereafter she shall not be ashamed to confess the faith of Christ crucified, and manfully to fight under His banner against sin, the world, and the devil ; and to continue Christ's faithful soldier and servant unto her life's end." The Godfathers and Godmothers are desired to take care that the child is brought to the Bishop to be confirmed, so soon as she can say the Creed, the Lord's Prayer, and the Ten Commandments, and is further instructed in the Church Catechism set forth for that purpose. The Catechism is the same for boys and girls. It teaches them their duty towards God and towards their neighbour in identical terms, with no suggestion of a different ideal for the two sexes. The Order of Confirmation follows on the same lines, and at the sacred rite of the Lord's Supper, men and women worship together, meeting on the ground of common humanity which underlies distinctions of sex.

In taking this line, our Church is surely following the teaching of Christ, as reported in the Gospels, which nowhere sets before women a distinctively feminine standard of conduct or enjoins them to confine their activity to a special sphere. So far as I can remember, only one instance is recorded of our Lord's rebuking a woman, and in that case the admonition was addressed to one who was too exclusively occupied by household cares, while at the same time her sister was commended for choosing the better part, though it involved what might have been regarded as neglect of home duties.

"The Spectator" and the Anti-Suffrage League approve of the part that women are taking in local Government as Guardians of the Poor, Town Councillors, &c. Does not the occupation of such posts often involve "struggle and battle"? Women on Boards of Guardians and elsewhere have fought manfully against the forces of ignorance, apathy, jobbery, and corruption. Will it be said that the conflict has left traces upon them which none can see without regret? Is it not rather the fact, that the impression produced by the patient, persevering and beneficent work of these women and their high personal character, has gone far in preparing the way for a reform which, it is believed, would add to their powers of usefulness?

That there are natural distinctions of sex is a fact which no rational person disputes, but to lay stress upon them as justifying separate moral ideals and an artificial demarcation of spheres of action, seems to be contrary both to Christian doctrine and the lessons of every-day experience.